Book Description

The rise of social media has created alternative methods of advertising for companies. Gone are the days where companies would reach their customers through newspapers or television commercials. It is now more affordable to connect with customers through online channels such as social media platforms. Companies have done an impressive job following their customers and establishing their brands within the same platforms that their customers enjoy. However, over the years, there have been questions surrounding brand trust, with many consumers challenging the authenticity of the message shared by brands.

There has been significant research compiled regarding customer sentiments on brand communication. One of the main insights found was that customers trusted messages shared by their peers over messages shared by brands. The assumption is that companies have an agenda to make profits, but our peers seek to educate and empower us. This key assumption is one of the driving forces, which has led to the growth of influencer marketing. Influencer marketing allows ordinary individuals to promote the services and products of companies to their specific target audience. Companies pay to have an influencer with a large following on popular social media platforms to advertise their offerings on their behalf. This business strategy has dramatically increased companies' return on investment (ROI) and helped build brand integrity among customers.

This book will be a valuable resource to all those individuals who are interested in becoming social media influencers. The reader will learn the ins and outs of social media marketing and some exclusive tactics and strategies on using social media platforms such as Facebook, Instagram, YouTube, TikTok, and Pinterest to develop and grow an audience. Readers will also learn how to create authentic personal brands that will help attract companies, provide them with a unique positioning in the market, and monetize their social media accounts. After reading this book, readers will feel motivated to capitalize on this new movement toward influencer marketing and begin to operate their own marketing enterprises.

Influencer Marketing for Beginners and Social Media Secrets

Your Guide to Building a Successful Personal Brand Using YouTube, Instagram, Facebook, TikTok & Pinterest

Adrian Peck

© Copyright 2020 - All rights reserved.

The content contained within this book may not be reproduced, duplicated or transmitted without direct written permission from the author or the publisher.

Under no circumstances will any blame or legal responsibility be held against the publisher, or author, for any damages, reparation, or monetary loss due to the information contained within this book, either directly or indirectly.

Legal Notice:

This book is copyright protected. It is only for personal use. You cannot amend, distribute, sell, use, quote or paraphrase any part, or the content within this book, without the consent of the author or publisher.

Disclaimer Notice:

Please note the information contained within this document is for educational and entertainment purposes only. All effort has been executed to present accurate, up to date, reliable, complete information. No warranties of any kind are declared or implied. Readers acknowledge that the author is not engaged in the rendering of legal, financial, medical or professional advice. The content within this book has been derived from various sources. Please consult a licensed professional before attempting any techniques outlined in this book.

By reading this document, the reader agrees that under no circumstances is the author responsible for any losses, direct or indirect, that are incurred as a result of the use of the information contained within this document, including, but not limited to, errors, omissions, or inaccuracies.

Table of Contents

Introduction
Chapter 1: The Rise of Digital Marketing
    Social Media and Customer Engagement
        Customer Value Journey
    Strategies for Finding and Engaging with Your Target Audience
    Exercise: Creating a Customer Avatar Profile
Chapter 2: Becoming the Brand: How to Create Your Personal Brand on Social Media
    Personal Brand Building
        Becoming a Storyteller
    The Importance of Building a Media Kit
        How to Find Like-Minded Partners and Brands
    Personal Brand Checklist
Chapter 3: How to Market Your Brand on YouTube
    How to Stand Out in Your Specific Niche
        Growing your Brand through Cross-Promotions and Collaborations
    Learning How to Create Appealing Banner Designs and Edit YouTube Videos
    The Basic Housekeeping Rules for using YouTube
Chapter 4: How to Market Your Brand on Instagram
    Building and Engaging with Your Instagram Community
        Guidelines for Brand Collaborations and Sponsored Posts
    The Effectiveness of Using Mixed Media
    Tips to Increase Content Engagement on Instagram
Chapter 5: How to Market Your Brand on Facebook
    Creating Shareable Content on Facebook
    Strategies for SEO
    How to Use Facebook Ads to Boost Sales and Traffic
        How to Create a Look-alike Audience
Chapter 6: How to Market Your Brand on Pinterest

    Using Pinterest to Drive Traffic to Your Brand

    The Anatomy of a Successful Pin

    A Complete Pinterest Strategy for Influencers

Chapter 7: How to Market Your Brand on TikTok

    Using "For You" Page to Your Benefit

    Setting Up Influencer Marketing on TikTok

        Strategies to Increase Follower Count

    Creating a TikTok Trend

Chapter 8: How to Pitch to Companies

    The Influencer - Brand Relationship

    Pitching to Brands

        Influencer Pitch Templates

    Common Mistakes to Avoid When Pitching to Brands

Chapter 9: How to Monetize Your Social Media Accounts

    Monetizing Your YouTube Page

    Monetizing Your Instagram Page

    Monetizing Your Facebook Page

    Monetizing Your Pinterest Page

    Monetizing Your TikTok Page

Chapter 10: Targeting Different Demographics with Different Social Media Platforms

    How to Find Your Target Audience Online

        Social Media User Demographics Per Social Media Platform

    Tactics on How to Locate Your Target Audience

Conclusion

    Take Charge of Your Message

References

Introduction

The age of the Internet has revolutionized how ordinary individuals engage with brands. I remember decades ago when the radio was the main medium that companies used to advertise their businesses and connect to their customers. In essence, if your company did not have a slot on a radio station, no one knew about it, and therefore, no one cared. Fast track to when the television was invented and marketers saw an opportunity to expand their audience reach by advertising brands on TV. This was the era of the most iconic commercials ever produced in our time; the commercials content was directly targeted at the desired customer and the call to action was crisp and clear.

For many years companies relied on traditional marketing mediums such as radio, television, and newspapers to spread the message about who they are and why their customers should support them. I do not believe that any marketer could have anticipated the digital wave that would follow in the early 2000s which would ultimately shift the marketing landscape for good. It all started with an invention known as the World Wide Web, which was conceived in 1991 by a programmer named Tim Berners-Lee. The purpose of the World Wide Web was to create an Internet that was not merely used as a platform to share files from one computer to another but was built to host a web of national and international information that anyone with access to it could retrieve.

Once the invention was established, individuals, researchers, and companies hurried to place their mark online and improve upon this technology by creating their own digital assets. In 1992, students from the University of Illinois partnered with researchers to develop an intelligent browser initially known as Mosaic. This was later renamed to Netscape, which offered a straightforward and user-friendly way of searching the Internet and using clickable links while viewing images and words on the same web page. Within the same year of this technological development, the American Congress supported the use of the Internet for commercial purposes. All of a sudden, companies were not limited to traditional platforms for marketing their brands—they could now create their own digital websites, blogs, or list their companies on popular online directories. It also allowed for a new type of entrepreneur—the e-commerce entrepreneur—to list and sell products online to a worldwide audience.

Today, digital marketing is one of the most powerful methods of communication that any company can use. This is because while traditional media could target a community or region, digital marketing can target a global audience. For instance, when targeting young people, marketers can now increase their reach from targeting millions within their state to reaching billions across the world. To effectively target the right group of people, companies have had to research the most effective strategies of engaging with their customers online. One of the most prevalent insights that have been found relating to customer engagement is that peers trust messages coming from their peers rather than being communicated by the companies or brands themselves. The major theme here is building customer trust, which is influenced not only by the message but by who is conveying the message.

Many consumers have become distrustful of brands whose messages sound forced or too staged. Over the years, celebrity endorsements have become disingenuous because most of the celebrities we see endorsing brands are paid to endorse the products (many of which they do not even use). The question of brand integrity is a significant one. To preserve it, many companies invest in influencer marketing as a strategic move away from shallow and disconnected advertising and toward a more authentic style of sharing their message. An influencer is an individual who has built a large social media following and subsequently leverages on their number of followers in advertising products and services for companies.

Influencer marketing has grown considerably over the years, and it is expected to continue rising each year. Seventeen percent of companies are already spending over half of their marketing budgets on influencer marketing because it is seen to bring an ROI that is similar to or at times better than other marketing channels. This industry's growth has created an opportunity for ordinary men and women to build their brands and make a living from marketing company brands. There is no better time than now to become an influencer because many companies are searching for people like you to carry their marketing portfolios and advertise their companies on their behalf. This book will teach you more about social media marketing and how to make the most out of social media tools and tactics. You will also learn how to create and monetize your brand and how to choose the most appropriate social media platform to reach your desired target audience.

This book offers all of the wisdom and knowledge that I have learned, serving as an entrepreneur and business coach. I will share with you all of the social media strategies and secrets I have exclusively shared with my clients and mentees about how to build an influential personal brand on Facebook, Instagram, YouTube, TikTok, or Pinterest. These strategies have made them millionaires, and now you have the opportunity to become one too. Decoding social media marketing is not difficult; however, it will take an open mind and a willingness to express your authentic persona to the world. I guarantee you that an individual like you would be best-suited to market a company's service or product. By the end of this book, you will have received all of the knowledge and exclusive tips on becoming a master at social media influencing. Therefore, without any more time wasted, let us learn a new skill that will open new doors of revenue and career experience for you!

Chapter 1: The Rise of Digital Marketing

Digital marketing can be defined as the process of promoting and selling a company's products or services through the use of online marketing tactics and strategies. It is perhaps one of the most powerful tools used by companies to give their brands the necessary exposure that they need and to connect with their customers online. The move to digital became essential with the social media boom of the 21st century, which has caused a migration from traditional marketing channels to embracing newer digital channels—such as social media—in getting the company's brand message across to a wider pool of prospects and customers.

One of the golden rules of marketing is always presenting the correct offer, at the most convenient time and in the most suitable place. Juggling all of these elements is a challenge for marketing teams; however, we can always bank on finding our customers online. The Internet is an indispensable part of our lives, from checking our social media feeds, reading articles online, receiving inspiration from our favorite blogs, or running online searches. Digital marketing allows companies to gain a share of our attention online. It places company brands within social media platforms, blogs, and news-sharing websites. This allows customers to engage with brands as part of their online experience and learn more about their products and services in real-time.

Digital marketing has revolutionized the marketing industry by allowing companies to build mutually beneficial relationships with their customers. It would be unreasonable to believe that a company's customers' needs will not change over time. As the customer matures and is exposed to newer technologies, shifts in lifestyle, and alternative forms of work, their attitude, behaviors, and values will change. Digital marketing provides companies with an opportunity to reach their customers, speak their language, and be a part of their ever-changing lives more naturally and intimately.

It also recognizes that modern customers begin their discovery and research into a brand online. It starts with a simple online search for a solution to their problem. This search leads to a website, social media page, reviews site, or articles providing the customer with more information. Their ultimate decision to contact a business is based on the useful information that they read online, the quality of business reviews, and the personal testimonials shared by family members or friends on social media or through word of mouth.

Therefore, I believe that every successful company should have a well-considered digital marketing plan that will help the organization in creating awareness of the number of services and products it offers and establish the company's brand in the customer's mind. Furthermore, it will allow companies to target new buyers who may have never had an experience with their brand before. These new buyers can become enthusiastic fans of the company, the more they learn about the business and personally engage with the brand. In essence, the gap between company and customer reduces significantly when a virtual relationship is built between the two parties and nurtured over time by sharing the right offers at the most appropriate time.

Social Media and Customer Engagement

One of the most incredible benefits of social media for companies is its potential to offer and facilitate customer engagement. Engagement here refers to the act of consumers opening up, expressing themselves, and participating in a social environment. Today's type of engagement is very different from the one-directional, read-only engagement that traditional media is known for. Social media engagement takes on a different tone and style; customers are now encouraged to participate actively instead of being mere viewers. The ideal scenario in a social media context would be a level of customer engagement that allows individuals to speak directly to companies and talk about companies among their social media circles in a way that positively impacts on the company's brand reputation.

Therefore, the customer engagement process is crucial for successful social media marketing and for companies to establish a powerful presence in the lives of their prospects and customers. Without evidence of engagement, we cannot measure whether customers are interested in the company or not; we do not know whether they love the company's products and are willing to purchase them. This would undoubtedly place the company in a predicament: do they continue to sell their products in a particular market or not? If our businesses are built to serve customers, then we should know if we are serving them to the best of our ability and according to their needs.

Companies are looking for conversations based on their products and services. The more people talk about a product, the greater its likeability and subsequently, its performance in the market. Many of us underestimate the importance of a simple compliment or expression of interest from a potential customer. When customers share their thoughts about an organization, they effectively become a part of the organization's marketing campaign. Now, the company must work to convert this potential customer into one that purchases products frequently from the company. Companies build their engagement strategies on the conversations they have with customers, which provide some much-needed guidance on how to structure their messages and present their service and product offerings. Nowadays, it is the customer who sets the tone and style of the message by being vocal about what they desire from the company's brand.

So what kind of conversations are companies willing to pay for? Well, I would say any product or service feature, function, or value that would catch the prospective or loyal customer's attention. Some companies would appreciate conversations occurring among four people, and other companies are not satisfied until millions of people are speaking about some element of their business. These conversations would allow the company to enter the conversation and engage in meaningful dialogue with their customers. Companies will even leverage on negative discussions and treat them as valuable moments to connect with their customers. For instance, someone may post on Facebook, "Ordered a meal from company X today, and my food arrived an hour late. So annoyed." The company's marketing team monitoring Facebook could comment, "Hey Mike! We know how annoying it can be to eat cold food. We want to make sure that your next meal is piping hot so we'll give you a coupon for your next order. DM us!"

Customer Value Journey

All digital marketing strategies begin and end with an in-depth analysis of the customer value journey. The customer value journey describes a process that every prospective buyer will go through before purchasing a company's product or service. This journey creates a build-up to the moment when a cautious consumer becomes a willing and enthusiastic customer. The journey from stranger to a friend is built through establishing a relationship with the consumer and providing all of the necessary information about the company that will help them uncover the value of the brand.

Thus, all of the company's digital marketing efforts are to facilitate this journey and make it flow as smoothly as possible without losing many potential customers along the way. There are eight stages involved in this journey, which immediately shows us that the process is not necessarily easy. Every stage must carefully consider the customer and ways in which the company can effectively connect with the customer in every single step. Remember that within the customer value journey, there will be a lot of communication between the company and the potential customer. This communication occurs using a range of digital marketing tactics. The frequency, consistency, and authenticity of the communication in each stage of the journey will be a multiplier of a company's success.

Stage 1: Building Awareness

No one can support a company that they are not aware of even exists. The first stage involves building awareness of the service or product offerings of the business. In essence, potential customers need to understand why they need a company such as the one presented in their lives. At first, nobody knew what Apple was about; however, over the years, the company has built such a powerful brand that customers are sleeping in queues so that they can be the first to get their hands on a new Apple product. Therefore, small companies do not need to be discouraged or overwhelmed regarding the task at hand because all major corporations began with only a handful of customers.

Stage 2: Engage with Your Prospects

Now that the prospective customers know that the company exists, the company moves from being a stranger to an acquaintance. It has not yet formed a relationship with the consumer, nor has the company built a level of familiarity or trust. Therefore, the goal in this stage is to engage with the prospect and develop a relationship. Many companies usually mess up when it comes to this part because they forget how normal relationships unfold. When we build a relationship with an acquaintance, we do not try to force relatability or convince them to purchase our merchandise.

Relationships built with a hidden agenda usually do not last because eventually, the agenda will be exposed. Instead, we need to start with basic information such as sharing who we are, what we value, our vision, and how we desire to make an impact in the world. Anyone can relate with ambition, values, and beliefs—and by "anyone," I am referring to the prospective customers. The engagement will continue to grow over time and become more personal, offer benefits, and yes, promote products and services.

Stage 3: Guide the Prospect toward Subscribing

Once the company's brand has made its mark, and the company continues to engage with prospective customers through shared content, it would be appropriate for the company to request customer contact details. At this point, this request would not seem awkward or creepy because some level of familiarity forms. When a company fails to capture prospective customers' details to continue communicating with them through other marketing channels, the company would have lost a potentially loyal future customer. The truth is that the customer becomes confronted with marketing messages from a plethora of companies every single day. If this company misses the opportunity of making a memorable impression, they will probably never hear from the customer ever again.

In other words, we cannot assume that a customer who reads a company's Facebook post will visit their Facebook page or make any further contact with that company. When there is no presence of a call-to-action such as the call to subscribe, follow, share, or comment, it is unlikely that the customer will engage any further with the post.

Companies can request prospective customers to subscribe by offering a free gift that is retrievable when the individual shares their email address. This exchange of value with information is known as an "ethical bribe." It is an effective strategy in allowing companies to grow their subscriber lists.

Stage 4: Conversion from Prospective Customer to Customer

Our success in stage three is influential in our stage four agenda of converting our potential customer into repeat customers. Stage three is only successful when our prospective customers, who are now on our subscriber list, remain engaged with the company. Thus as time goes by, they naturally increase their level of commitment. Of course, these prospective customers would only increase their commitment when the content shared by the company continues to offer value in the form of education, advice, inspiration, the sharing of skills or support. This stage can be nerve-wrecking for any company owner because they need to trust in the investment that they have put into building a relationship with the prospect to pay off.

To reduce the anxiety involved in this stage, companies should not expect to start making a profit from their prospect. At this stage of the game, the only expectation should be to increase the prospect's engagement with the company's brand and spend more time asking questions, commenting, liking, or reposting the company's content. This stage proves the fact that most successful businesses in the world know to be true: customer acquisition is an extremely costly marketing exercise that the business will undertake because victory at this point in the customer journey is not assured. Yet, the company must continue to invest in winning the prospective customer.

Stage 5: Create Excitement

By stage 5, the prospective customer has made a transaction with the company, even if it was a small transaction. The company's efforts at this stage are focused on making sure that the excitement does not end after the transaction is made. In other words, the company needs to ensure that the purchase carries a ripple effect of value. When the customer does not hear from the company after the sale goes through or they are not encouraged to purchase another product, the company will never hear from them again. At this stage, the customer has not been won yet and thus the relationship requires more sustained nurturing. Therefore, part of creating excitement involves curating valuable buying experiences that always have an after-sale or follow-up engagement involved. The greater the value the company offers, the more willing the customer will be to try out new products or increase the amount of time or money spent on the company.

Stage 6: Time to Rise

Most companies would have spent thousands of dollars acquiring a customer at this point in the journey. By stage six, they would have already spent a significant amount of time and money without making a considerable amount of profit. This can be a stressful position to be in, considering that the company is operating in a highly competitive market. However, the cost of acquiring customers becomes an investment toward future returns and profits from the nurtured and loyal customers. The good news is that at stage six, customers are willing to purchase a greater amount of products or pick the expensive subscriptions or memberships. This is also the stage where most companies will present their main offer to the customer. Once the customer has purchased this main offer, the company can now sell all of the other complimentary offers.

Stage 7: Advocate

Every company wants to reach stage seven because, at this stage, the company has happy customers who are eager to spend their money weekly, monthly, or annually on a company's products or services. At this stage, the customer knows what the company stands for and can clearly express the value that the company brings into their lives. The company then focuses its efforts on creating shareable content that allows the customers to become advocates of the company. A brand advocate is an individual who has had a positive experience with the company brand and desires to share their feedback, reviews, and sentiments about the company with their peers.

I like to think of a brand advocate as a promoter that you do not have to pay. They will willingly offer advice on approaching and purchasing products and services from their favorite companies because of how much value they have received from the company over the years. These positive reviews are golden for the company because they allow prospective customers to approach the company with a willingness to cooperate and engage in receiving further information and knowledge-sharing.

Stage 8: Promote! Promote! Promote!

Company promoters differ from brand advocates because promoters are paid by the company to spread marketing messages regarding the company's products or services. Promoters, therefore, have a wider net in drawing prospective customers toward the company; their messages are intentional and carried out to bring positive attention to the company. There is always an incentive that companies will give to promoters (sometimes in the form of money and other times in the form of discounts or merchandise) for the promoter to leverage their fan base, social media following, networks with friends and family, or their reputation, in promoting the company brand.

Many companies love to use promoters because a new audience is hearing about the company's product or service from a familiar and trusted source. This means that the message is not treated with suspicion or indifference, as it sometimes is when a company carries out its own promotions. The new audience is excited to share in the same experience as their trusted source, and the decision to purchase a product or service from the company becomes easy and filled with excitement. I find that prospective customers are more likely to become repeat customers when their first impression of the company comes from hearing about a positive review or experience from a relative or a close friend.

Strategies for Finding and Engaging with Your Target Audience

The worst marketing advice anyone can give is to chase profits and forget about anything else. If companies were marketing to robots, perhaps I would agree with this kind of advice; however, they are selling to real people who live real lives full of highs and lows and everything in between. Companies would be erroneous to place all of their efforts in growing email lists or their social media following without considering the one metric that would allow them to receive a wave of support, paying customers or followers online. This metric is known as engagement, and it can effectively boost a company's brand by over 300% (Bullas, 2017).

Great customer engagement is all about the quality that a customer receives when they land on a website, social media page, or stumble across a sponsored post. This quality is an offering of value, which can cause them to bookmark a web page or add products onto their wish list to revisit the company page at a later date. Below are useful strategies for increasing audience engagement and creating a digital environment where customers desire to do business with the company.

1. **Know Where Your Customers Are**

One of the best ways of understanding what customers want is to understand how they live, their interests, and where they prefer to spend most of their time on the Internet. Companies wouldn't have an effective digital marketing strategy if they shared content on a platform that their audience did not frequently use. Even if their content were great, they would not experience the kind of results that they would hope for. Therefore, companies need to conduct some research, find out where their customers are, and how they prefer to communicate.

2. **Know What Your Customers Are Looking For**

People do not just find a company website or social media page by accident (there are too many active social media accounts for anyone to stumble on a page). Instead, new visitors find a company page due to the quality of content that the company shares. This means that new visitors or customers relate to a company's content before establishing a relationship with them. If the content is not engaging, the chances are that visitors will ignore their post or offer. Therefore, companies need to know what their audience is looking for to create relevant and tailored content. Some of the ways that they can share relevant content are to answer pertinent questions or provide solutions to a problem that their targeted audience has. Another way for them to deliver relevant content is to share knowledge or insights that are new and appropriate to the phase of life that their audience is currently in. Companies need to find ways of adding value in the lives of their target audience—who already receive many offers and requests every day.

3. Remain Consistent and Always Reliable

A customer's relationship with a company is very volatile, especially when it is still new. Remember that it takes time and other forms of investment to maintain a relationship with customers. Furthermore, a company's engagement declines when it cannot commit to a consistent routine or system in communicating with those it seeks to serve. Just because a company manages to win its audience's attention it does not necessarily mean that it will keep it indefinitely. Therefore, I believe that consistency is key; by this, I mean that anything the company commits must occur for the entire term or the duration planned for it. For instance, if the company plans to post two articles a week for a 3-month campaign, it must commit to posting two articles on the days and times they scheduled it for. Moreover, a company's consistency creates a community of followers who prioritize consuming the company's content whenever it is available. Sooner or later, the company creates advocates who are willing to repost or share the company's content whenever it is released.

4. Be Sure to Measure and Optimize Your Shared Content

The main goal of creating content is to kickstart the customer value journey or convert prospective customers into loyal customers. Therefore, most of the time, companies create content that is packed with keywords, images, and an overall message, which encourages the audience to further engage with the brand. It is the company's responsibility to monitor the performance of its content by tracking the social media page or website's statistical data. This data will provide necessary information about strong and weak content and how clear the content's message or instruction was to the customer (it shows whether the customer followed through with the request made in the message).

I would also recommend that companies understand which metrics they are tracking to provide structure and clear goals to digital marketing campaigns. Companies can also optimize their content to engage with their audience and, thus, receive better traction. Optimizing content requires an in-depth understanding of one's target audience so that the message reflects their unique experiences and needs. The data collected from social media pages or websites can also help the company create a meaningful content strategy targeted to specific groups of people.

Exercise: Creating a Customer Avatar Profile

Digital marketing is not about selling everything to everyone. We need to select a group of individuals we believe are the most suitable customers for our product or service. In the business sense, companies are looking for deeper connections and conversions through their content. Therefore, they need to identify and target the correct kind of prospects. When we understand who our target audience is, we can easily locate them online. Creating a customer avatar profile is an exercise that will help us profile an average member of our target audience who would represent the collective values, lifestyle, and interests of our entire audience.

The customer avatar is fictitious; however, it will allow us to gain a good idea of how our ideal customer would live. We should include as much detail as possible when creating this profile because it will impact on the quality of our messaging and marketing tactics. Therefore, we need to paint a picture of a typical customer and their specific desires, social behaviors, interests, fears, and dreams. After completing this profile, you will gain a better understanding of your ideal customer, their motivations to support your company, their expectations from the company's brand, and what kind of offer they would find appealing.

Step 1: Create Your Customer Avatar

The quickest way to start building your customer avatar profile is to understand your ideal customer's demographic traits. This includes essential information about the identity of your customer. On a piece of paper, provide answers related to the following life segments:

- ☐ Age range
- ☐ Sex
- ☐ Occupation
- ☐ Geographical location
- ☐ Highest level of education
- ☐ Relationship status

- ☐ Income bracket
- ☐ Household size

Once you have written the demographic traits of your ideal customer, you can now write down the psychographic traits. Psychographic traits refer to the behaviors that motivate customers to make purchasing decisions. Answer some of these questions based on your ideal customer's buying psychology:

- ☐ What are their hobbies or social interests? (Is your customer a foodie or avid reader?)
- ☐ What kind of lifestyle do they live? (Are they a workaholic or perhaps a vegan?)
- ☐ What are your customer's core values? (What principles do they live by?)
- ☐ What are some of their personal goals? (Do they want to lose weight or perhaps become wealthy?)
- ☐ What kind of social causes does your customer support? (Are they an animal activist, or do they support gender equality?)
- ☐ What existing brands does your customer use as part of their lifestyle? (These do not have to be your competitors; however, they may include them).

Step 2: Describe Your Customer's Pain Points

We can only serve our customers when we know what factors they might be struggling with. In this step, I would like you to create a list of four or five realistic and genuine challenges that your customer is likely to be experiencing based on their customer avatar that you have just created. This step allows you to understand your customer's pain points so that the communication between you can be more empathetic and relatable.

You can complete this step by conducting primary research by collecting statistical data or through secondary research by conducting surveys or receiving feedback from your audience. For instance, if your company was a beauty brand, your customer's pain point might be, "I can never find a foundation that matches my skin tone." Or if your company offered a cleaning service, its customer's pain point might be, "I barely find time to clean my home with all of the demands placed on me in my life."

Step 3: Identify How You Can Solve Their Pain Points

This final step will help you identify the goals or results that your ideal customer would receive by doing business or interacting with you. In other words, it will help you create a unique sales position that would offer customers value that they cannot receive from any other company. To complete this step effectively, think of perfect scenarios that would remedy all of the challenges that appear in step two. Essentially, your outcomes need to propose a positive solution for turning their pain into joy. For instance, in the first example, the ideal scenario in doing business with the beauty company would be if it offered access to makeup that matches all skin tones and improves the overall health of all skin types.

Chapter 2: Becoming the Brand: How to Create Your Personal Brand on Social Media

In the previous chapter, I introduced you to digital marketing and how it has helped companies reach their target audience in ways that were impossible before the dawn of the Internet. I discussed the customer value journey, which detailed the steps that companies will take in engaging with prospective customers to win them over and turn them into loyal customers. Now that you understand how companies use digital marketing as an effective marketing tool, it is time that I show you where you fit in. This book is all about how you can leverage on your influence online to help companies source and convert prospective customers into loyal and enthusiastic brand advocates.

To become a sought-after promoter who is paid thousands of dollars for a simple sponsored post, you will need to understand how to become a brand and use similar customer engagement tactics to build your community of followers on social media platforms. Before you can be known as an influencer, you must first build a brand for yourself that will allow you to attract an audience who can relate to or support your lifestyle, interests, and values. I believe that in the world, there are natural-born leaders and natural-born followers.

As an influencer, you will become a leader in your particular niche and lead a community of followers who receive value from the content that you choose to create and share. As an influencer with a unique personal brand, you will use digital marketing similarly to how companies use digital marketing. However, your revenue will come from promoting products and services that are relatable to your particular lifestyle and which provide some level of value to your followers. For an influencer, their personal brand is their largest asset. When nurtured and built correctly, it can become a valuable commodity that companies will pay to be associated with.

Personal Brand Building

Take a minute to reflect on some pertinent questions about yourself. Consider the following:

1. What word best describes me?

2. What would others say about me?
3. What skills or talents differentiate me from my peers?

Your personal brand becomes the sum of all of these questions. The truth is that you have a reputation whether you are conscious of it or not. This reputation can be positive, negative, or neutral, depending on how much effort you have invested in curating your brand identity. Your brand identity consists of factors that you cannot control, such as your heritage, culture, or past experiences; and factors that you can control, such as your experience, skills, personality, and behaviors. Your identity forms a brand that becomes your spoken or unspoken message you will share with your friends, family members, or the general public.

Think about the experience of meeting someone for the first time. Within 390 milliseconds, you would have already formed some kind of perception about the individual and their personality or attitude. It may have been a small aspect of the individual's personality that made you come to your conclusion; for instance, their tone of voice, facial expressions, or body language. Your first impression of the individual may not have been a true representation of who they are. However, due to our short attention span as human beings, you wouldn't have continued the conversation long enough to reveal their genuine personality. I always emphasize the importance of first impressions because, in all honesty, people connect to the message that we are putting across before they can get to know who we really are.

Building a strong personal brand requires you to take full ownership of the messages that you are constantly sharing with others knowingly or unknowingly. You need to start seeing yourself as the CEO of the most successful company: Me Ltd. This means that your personal advancement in life will depend on how well you can market yourself to others and promote your causes and agendas. For example, becoming an influencer will require an understanding of who you are and the value you have to offer others. Perhaps you are great at baking, and you want to share dessert recipes with an online audience; or maybe you are a lover of fast cars, and you want to offer reviews and other educational material to people similar to you online. Regardless of your interests, your personal brand will help you create a convincing message that will draw the appropriate crowd of followers and business partners.

What you sell as an influencer will always be in demand because you will always find a community of people interested in similar interests and hobbies. However, your talents or hobbies will be of no use when you do not have a clear strategy on how you desire to build and manage your brand (as well as in managing and influencing how others perceive you). Ultimately, a powerful personal brand will conjure three standard perceptions (which you can use to fuel your brand). Firstly, it will convince others that you are different. Your target audience will see you as a refreshing addition to their social media feed, and your perceived originality will translate as being valuable or indispensable.

Secondly, your personal brand will convince others that you are better than the other brands that they have previously seen. Let's face it—all of us want to be associated with someone more successful or learned than we are because it allows us to acquire new skills or feel more accomplished than we are. Strong personal brands promote the belief that the individual is in a league of their own and, therefore, worthy of our attention. Lastly, a strong personal brand will convince others that you are authentic. It is very difficult to fake authenticity because human beings have a natural sixth sense or intuitive mind which can separate the real from the phony. Furthermore, your authenticity will allow you to promote other brands with a level of genuineness, encouraging your followers to believe in the features, benefits, or advantages of using a company's products or services.

Becoming a Storyteller

Human beings are naturally great storytellers because of how unique our life experiences are and the various ways that we choose to express our existence. Our expression of who we are and why we believe that we are special is, in essence, telling a story. My story will be different from yours because of the different life experiences we have lived through and our different motivations in life. I believe that there is always room for another story to be shared with others and strategically leveraged to build healthy relationships between people.

You may not think that you have a great story to share or that you are not a great storyteller; however, every day you engage in an internal dialogue with yourself and the outcomes of this dialogue shape your entire existence—so do you think that your stories are not influential? Creating a brand story that we can share with others can be done by simply developing a narrative that will allow us to share a meaningful message with our audience and empower them to take action somehow. Your narrative will consist of information that is structured in a way that makes your message memorable and relatable to your target audience.

Your brand story will be shared on your social media platforms and continuously inserted in your content until the narrative resonates with those you seek to connect with. In creating a meaningful brand story, there are three elements you need to consider; each element describes an aspect of the overall story that adds value to your personal brand. I recommend that you share all three aspects with your target audience through well-considered messages. The first element of a brand story is the meta-narrative, which includes information about your values, beliefs, purpose, and long-term vision. You will also have the opportunity to differentiate yourself from other personal brands by stating your unique selling point and your personal strengths that make you the best person to promote a specific company brand.

The second element of a brand story is the macro-narrative, which contains information about your identity; who you are, what you enjoy doing, and what you can offer other brands. Essentially, the macro-narrative includes a summary of your biography and all the unique factors that make you such an original. Most of the time, we will see influencers include elements of a macro-narrative on their social media profiles, blog bios, or websites. This type of information helps to encourage others to learn more about who they are in a more personal manner.

The third element of a brand story is the micro-narrative which includes daily messages that you will share on your social media platforms that will effectively reinforce your macro and meta narratives. There are a variety of ways that you can share micro-stories that will reaffirm your interests, lifestyle, and show a lot of personality. The goal of the micro-narrative is to encourage \ your target audience to engage with your brand and share your content (to build brand advocates).

Your brand story will travel further than you could ever go. This carefully crafted message has the potential to touch lives and resonate with people from across the world. Companies and other brands approach an influencer after having had an encounter with their messages. During the early stages of building your personal brands, you will need to spend time thinking about what you want to be known for and what kind of stories you would like your audience to share. It is important to remember that you are in control of your own narrative. Therefore, it is your responsibility to make sure that what others are sharing about you is what you have intended for them to communicate.

The Importance of Building a Media Kit

One of the surest signs in knowing that companies consider an influencer to be noteworthy is when companies ask to present an influencer media kit. I always find that influencers are unprepared for this moment. Most of the time, they have not organized any form of documentation regarding their personal brand or target audience outreach. Truthfully speaking, there are so many personal brands on various social media platforms, and when an influencer is unprepared for an opportunity, companies will simply move along to the next available person

Therefore, I strongly recommend that all people who work in the creative arts, must consider building their own media kit and continue curating their unique portfolio of work through their social media pages, blogs, or creative websites. I say this because when creative people continue to produce and publish quality work and their work gains the necessary traction, they may soon be classified as influencers and personally scouted by brands.

When brands approach an influencer through email, social media platforms, or influencer networks, they will initially request a document known as a media kit to assess whether the influencer will be a good fit for their brand and determine how large the influencer's network is. I would describe an influencer media kit as playing a similar role to a resume. Similarly to a resume, an influencer media kit will tell the brand important information about how you can be of value to them. This would include information, such as who you are, what your interests are, your particular target audience, and what you could offer the brand. This document gives the influencer the chance to sell their unique message and show brands how impactful their online content creation is.

Influencer media kits that are sent to potential clients must be designed professionally while also showcasing the influencer's personality and creativity in how it is formatted and structured. It is okay to have fun playing around with color schemes, fonts, and images that would help you express your personal brand in the most authentic way possible. Influencers also need to keep their media kits brief, only including relevant and factual data, highlighting the strengths of the influencer. Paying attention to the smaller details like grammar or spelling mistakes will also help the influencer deliver a clean and well-presented document. In the event that they decide to use imagery, it is important that the influencer make sure that these images are of utmost quality and appropriately represent their personal brand.

While it is important to make this document beautiful, you cannot forget about the vital information that brands and potential partners want to see. Firstly, brands will want to know a little more about you (perhaps a more in-depth version of your online bio). It isn't necessary to tell brands your entire life history; instead, I believe influencers should focus on detailing their particular niche and the expertise that they have acquired in this field over the years. Brands will want to know whether they are partnering with an influencer whose brand aligns with theirs; thus, you can conduct research on the brand and include similar values that both of you share. Remember that your honesty will get you further in winning a brand over than embellishing your information would. Therefore, be yourself and allow your confidence and personality to reflect in the introductory section.

Once brands have been won over by your introduction, they will be eager to learn more about the statistics that your personal brand generates on a weekly or monthly basis. At the end of the day, brands are also companies, and as exciting as the partnership might be, they need to receive an ROI from using you as their promoter. One of the first figures they will look for is your number of followers. Even though this number does not show the full picture of your effectiveness, it is still useful in showing that you have a level of influence online. You can list the number of followers for each social media account and the overall number of followers from all platforms.

Brands will also look for other metrics such as the average number of page views, the number of times people click on your posts, or view your videos and the level of engagement that you receive from your shared content. Once a social media account switches to a business account or profile, it will have an analytics page that will detail all the necessary metrics that brands want to see. If you operate a website or a blog, I recommend that you insert an analytics plugin or alternatively, register for a free Google Analytics account that will track all of your site visits and how many times visitors engaged with your posts.

Some of the other relevant information to add to your media kit would be a summary of your target audience demographics, a summary of the past work experience that you have done for other brands, any current partnerships that you are a part of and testimonials from past brand partnerships that you have collaborated with. Lastly, you need to stipulate your rates for the various services that you are willing to offer brands in exchange for monetary compensation. I know how difficult or awkward it can be to decide on a payment rate, especially when you do not have any prior work experience as an influencer.

At the beginning of your career, you can offer your services in exchange for products or other merchandise. This will allow you to gain much-needed experience and work on building your credibility as an influencer. Eventually, you would have earned enough exposure and confidence to charge brands for the work that you perform on their behalf. On average, influencers will charge rates between $50 and $250,000 depending on their reach, audience equality, content quality, and the earned social media value (or reputation) of the influencer.

How to Find Like-Minded Partners and Brands

After compiling your media kit, you must decide on the best strategy of getting it in the hands of the brands you desire to partner with. Some influencers will choose to hold on to their media kit until a brand approaches them, and others will seek to find like-minded brands and connect with them. For those who will choose to send it out to potential partners, it is important to consider which brands to send it to carefully; it would be in the influencer's best interest to prioritize sending their media kits to brands that align with their own personal brand. This would provide the influencer with a greater opportunity of being contacted by the potential partner for further discussions.

There are three main options that you can choose when seeking to find brands online and connect with them. Connecting with a company does not need to be an overwhelming task. In most cases, companies are excited to receive new brand ambassadors who can help them showcase their brand to audiences worldwide. Therefore, it is worth looking for brands that would benefit from the value that you offer. The first option in finding brands is to look for them on influencer networks. An influencer network is simply a marketplace where creatives can go to connect with brands and pitch for upcoming campaigns and other opportunities. Both parties benefit from these kinds of networks because companies find talent and influencers can connect with the marketing departments of these companies.

The second option for finding brands is to look for them on other influencers' social media feeds. For instance, if you can see that a brand is sponsoring the influencer, you can assume that the brand is also working with other influencers on the same brand campaign. Once you know that a brand utilizes influencer marketing as one of its marketing strategies, it is a lot easier to approach the brand with your media kit and make your first impression meaningful.

Alternatively, the third option suggests that you make direct contact with the brand and make your offer to collaborate with them. Reaching out directly to brands is painless; usually, you will find contact details on their social media pages (alternatively, you can find contact information on their websites). From there, you will send them a direct message. The best department to contact in a company would be the sales and marketing department or the public relations department. In your professional email or direct message, you would introduce yourself and provide a summary of the information which brands will find detailed in your media kit. After that, you would sign off by letting the brand know how to contact you for further communication.

Personal Brand Checklist

A personal brand is a professional reputation that you desire to share with others. It refers to how you will choose to package your value message and talents. The stronger your personal brand becomes, the greater the level your credibility, online influence, and career opportunities you will acquire. Therefore, when you are building your personal brand, ensure that you have followed some of the tips and suggestions in this checklist below:

Personal Brand Checklist:

- ☐ **Google yourself and see what information comes up in the search results.** Most brands will conduct a quick Google search to learn more about you and assess the quality of your reputation. Make sure that you delete any images or posts on your social media that do not represent your brand in a positive light. Additionally, you should ensure that all of the information presented is factual and up-to-date.
- ☐ **Create a meaningful value proposition.** A value proposition highlights the distinct qualities, skills, and talents that you bring to the table. The value that you bring should always be authentic to who you are, and it should also represent what you stand for. A strong value proposition will also explain the purpose behind your craft as an influencer and the long-term vision to accomplish in your work.
- ☐ **Network to grow your brand.** Networking is vital, especially in the beginning stages of a personal brand. This is because you need to showcase your brand to partners and brands to gain the necessary recognition. Consider connecting with like-minded people within your niche industry on social media platforms like LinkedIn or Twitter. Alternatively, you can attend conferences and events that are related to what your brand stands for. Networking will help you build a strong community of followers and potential business clients who are willing to support your brand.
- ☐ **Create a website or a personal blog.** When influencers secure a significant amount of brand assets online, they are more likely to be located on search engines and increase their credibility in their field. Nowadays, a website or a blog works in the same way as a business card; it is an opportunity to present your personal brand and strikingly offer your value proposition. I also find that when influencers focus on generating content on their websites or blogs and share their content on their social media pages, it can boost the number of views or impressions that the content receives and positively increase traffic to their website or blog.
- ☐ **Live your brand online and offline.** Setting up social media accounts and ensuring that they are consistent with your brand is great; however, your brand cannot merely survive online. Your reputation as an influencer will be judged by how your online community perceives you and how the general public (those you interact with daily) perceive you.

Personal development should be a constant commitment on your journey to becoming a successful influencer. Your attitude toward life, your behavior toward others, and your physical appearance should all work together to reinforce who you say you are and the value you say you can offer. Therefore, consider your dress code, remember people's names, and always practice good etiquette—these simple acts will have a positive impact on your brand.

Chapter 3: How to Market Your Brand on YouTube

Video-sharing is perhaps one of the most influential tactics to use in digital marketing. As human beings, we are visual creatures, regarding visual stimulation being more pleasurable and memorable than written text or shared images. A video is also a powerful tool when used for storytelling; through videos, we can explain concepts more efficiently, give believable product reviews, and share our unique personalities with others. Over the years, there has been a rise in video-sharing due to the increase in access to the Internet, smarter technological devices, and improved internet connections.

YouTube is by far the most popular video-sharing platform globally, boasting of 2 billion registered users worldwide. This platform is a popular choice for video-streaming among the young and the old alike. Businesses have joined the YouTube community, with nearly 8 out of 10 (78.8%) of marketers considering the platform to be an effective marketing tool (Mohsin, 2020). YouTube has the power to increase a company's visibility among its video loving target audience. It provides opportunities for companies, such as car manufacturers or beauty brands, to easily share their current news and product updates and receive feedback from their customers through the YouTube comments.

Although many other social media platforms allow users to upload and share videos easily, many brands still prefer to share extended and more in-depth videos on social media channels like YouTube. I am yet to find another platform that gives brands the ability to demonstrate the use or function of a product or capture an individual's personality in such detail in an edited and content-rich YouTube video. Therefore, I find that YouTube is a great video-sharing platform, useful in sharing experiences and content that prompts engagement from the targeted audience.

Influencers can build their brands on YouTube by creating relatable video content that would allow viewers to buy into the brand and learn more about the influencer's value offer. The best way to gain a following on YouTube is to decide on a particular niche that you hope to dominate. After, take some time to view other people's channels who have already created a name for themselves in that specific niche. After conducting your research, you will see a gap within your niche that isn't occupied yet. This notable gap will become your unique value proposition, which you will leverage to build your personal brand. From then onwards, your task will be to create engaging content that explores various themes and topics related to your particular value offer. For instance, a beauty influencer may decide on creating content that primarily focuses on finding and testing organic skincare products for the various skin types. The multiplier of the beauty brand's success would be creating a meaningful brand on YouTube and producing shareable video content in their organic skincare products niche.

How to Stand Out in Your Specific Niche

Every YouTube influencer's dream is to produce content that trends or receives thousands of views per video. This is because trending content draws the attention of relevant brands, and it allows the influencer to generate an income (once the video reaches a certain threshold of views). Trending in one's specific niche is also an incredible milestone to achieve because it affirms the strength of the influencer's personal brand and ultimately allows them to achieve favorable analytical data on their channel, which would be advantageous when approaching brands for partnerships. Below is a list of strategies to help you receive the attention you deserve in your particular niche on YouTube.

1. **Post on YouTube Frequently and Consistently**

YouTube channels that commit to posting more than one video per week are known to perform higher than those who post sporadically and inconsistently. They are also more likely to receive recommended views. I would suggest that you post two to three videos per week as a new micro-influencer to grow your following and share your unique content online. You can go a step further and create a routine to create and publish video content on YouTube. This routine will help you establish a full library of content in no time, assisting you in improving your channel performance on YouTube's algorithm, and drive quality views to your channel.

2. **Create an Interesting Hook for Your Intro's**

Hooks are brilliant for introducing who you are and what your YouTube channel is all about in the first few opening seconds. They allow visitors to understand your brand and have a memorable jingle or sentence they can remember you by. However, not all hooks are about promoting your personal brand. Many YouTube influencers will use the hook to briefly summarize the video's content in an interesting way, which makes viewers stay tuned in to the video for longer. For instance, a YouTube channel that demonstrates how to assemble flatpack furniture could use the hook to show the viewer the finished piece of furniture already assembled. This short teaser would allow the viewer to continue watching to see the step-by-step process of how the hobbyist did it.

3. Keep Your Opening and Closing Sequence Short

I always recommend for YouTubers to keep their opening and closing sequences short for various reasons. This is because most viewers will lose interest after a few seconds. It is a known fact that our attention span as human beings has significantly reduced since the emergence of technologies such as social media, which provide overstimulation. In essence, we become bored fairly quickly and move on to the next interesting piece of content. Therefore, I would suggest that you keep your opening and closing sequence less than 10 seconds combined.

4. Boost Your Videos by Adding End Screens

End screens can significantly boost the traffic on your YouTube channel by allowing viewers to stay on your channel longer and engage with more of your video content. End screens are interactive graphics placed at the end of a video that provides a link to other related videos from the same YouTuber. For instance, if a viewer was watching a DIY video of how to assemble a study desk, the end screen would prompt them to watch another DIY video, from the same individual, showing them how to assemble a coffee table. It is up to the influencer to decide where the end screen will appear; however, it can only appear within the last 20 seconds of the video.

5. Create Different Types of Content

YouTube channels that only offer one type of content won't encourage viewers to become subscribers. Hence, I would recommend that influencers alternate between three types of content material by using the hub, hero, and help content strategy. These three content strategies serve three different goals and allow your community of subscribers to stay excited about new content releases. The hub strategy involves creating community-building video content that would encourage you to establish a greater relationship with your subscribers. Hub video content may focus on responding to viewer questions or feedback, sharing a personal story with your followers, or going live and opening the floor for random discussions and topics with your viewers.

The hero strategy involves creating videos that can be readily shared and recommended on YouTube or other social media platforms and blogs. These videos will focus on discussing relevant and trending topics such as breaking news, gossip, or social, political, and cultural transformations. Lastly, the help strategy involves creating videos with high searchable content. These videos will provide a solution or an explanation to a common problem, concept, or phenomenon that YouTube users search for regularly. For instance, help videos can provide actionable steps such as DIY videos, advice on solving a psychological or physical problem, or sometimes they can help viewers learn how to use or fix devices, equipment, and other accessories.

Growing your Brand through Cross-Promotions and Collaborations

Cross-promotion and collaborations help you gain more visibility by associating yourself with other like-minded brands on YouTube. They are also useful in introducing you to a new audience or potential subscribers who have not heard of your channel before. To simply put it, collaborations are videos that are created by a few content creators and shared on their respective channels to leverage on each creator's audience. It is a great strategy for micro-influencers who are just starting and would like to gain more exposure on YouTube. Think of it as being an endorsement of your brand to an untapped viewership. As instrumental as collaborations can be in gaining new subscribers, it will not guarantee that the traffic of visitors will fall in love with your channel and subscribe. Your overall channel art, quality of content, and video editing skills will play a significant role in convincing a visitor to convert to a subscriber.

One important consideration regarding collaborations is that you must choose a brand with a similar audience, but one that covers a different kind of niche. This will help you usher in new traffic of visitors to your channel who have not seen your type of content. YouTubers are always on the look-out for new and interesting channels offering information that they have not heard of before. Therefore, these new visitors are more likely to consider subscribing to your channel when they see your name or face pop up in their usual hang-out channels.

When choosing a YouTube brand to partner with, you should always aim for brands with a slightly larger following than yours or brands with a small following that is rapidly growing every month. The chances of a popular YouTube influencer agreeing to partner with a new micro-influencer are slim; therefore, approach those brands where both of you would receive mutual value. At the beginning of your YouTube journey, it should be your goal to form as many relationships with like-minded brands as possible. Even if you are not immediately reaping benefits from your relationships, it is always great to build a community that can offer you support and advice and eventually build mutually beneficial partnerships.

Learning How to Create Appealing Banner Designs and Edit YouTube Videos

There is a common theme among the most successful YouTube channels—all of them look visually appealing. Each video has a thumbnail that is eye-catching and suitable for the influencer's personal brand. It is as if the channel display conveys a strong message or story about the YouTube influencer. It is no wonder these channels can convert a visitor into a subscriber, only after a few minutes of perusing through their channel page. I want to show you how simple it is to create aesthetically pleasing YouTube banners that will allow those who are new to your brand to be encouraged to watch your video content and learn more about who you are.

The first advice I will give you is to make sure that the images you desire to use for your banner are readable on any device. It is common to find an image that looks great on an android device but stretched and disproportionate on a tablet or PC. One of the ways to standardize the look of your images on all devices is to follow YouTube's recommended dimensions for banners. According to YouTube (2020), the appropriate size for banners is 2560 pixels wide and 1440 pixels long.

Many websites offer YouTube banner templates that are in the correct size. All you would need to do is customize their template according to your brand colors, fonts, and images. Once you have designed your banner, you can download it on your device and upload it on your YouTube channel. One of the most trusted graphics websites that offers beautifully designed social media banners, including YouTube banners, is Canva. What I love about Canva is that it is extremely user-friendly; this means that you do not need to be a graphic designer to create an aesthetically pleasing project. Those who are looking to put in a minimal effort on their templates will find Canva templates convenient, and the fact that it is free to register an account and enjoy some of the website's benefits is a sweet incentive.

Another awesome website that allows influencers to play around with banner designs is Snappa. Similarly to Canva, Snappa will provide you with access to their 6000+ templates and millions of images and graphics to use when designing your banner. What I find interesting about Snappa is that their software shows the designer how their banner will sit on the YouTube channel and allows them to make the necessary provisions in case a portion of their image does not fit well into the frame. Although Snappa also offers a free subscription, it limits the user to only three downloads per month. Therefore, influencers who enjoy switching up their social media graphics will find Snappa's free offer to be quite restricting. Of course, both Canva and Snappa offer paid subscriptions that come with a plethora of features and benefits that will provide you with the tools of making your YouTube graphics look professionally designed.

Once you have chosen a design software, you are now at liberty to let your imagination run loose! Imagine yourself as a visitor on your channel and design your banner and logo in a way that creates your desired message. This is your time to make the best first impression through visual imagery. The first tip that I will give you is to remember to fill in the white gaps on the sides that are not part of the rectangle in the middle (the center of your banner). I would recommend that you create a complimentary background image to fill the space and ensure that your banner looks great on all devices. Secondly, when you are designing your banner, remember that YouTube will automatically add all of your social media links as an overlay. This means that your design should not include a lot of distracting information around the bottom right corner where your links will be located. You want visitors to see that your brand is present on other social media platforms, making it easier for them to follow you on other platforms.

Editing YouTube videos does not need to be a complicated process. I believe that the beginning stages of editing your video content allows you to think of all of the techniques and styles that you desire to use as a standard format for all of your videos going forward. Once you have figured out how all your videos should be formatted and all of the filters and icons that you will include in your videos, your editing job will become so much easier and go a lot quicker. Nonetheless, we cannot forget that video content is always about storytelling. This means that our edited videos should run smoothly and have a clearly defined introduction, body, and conclusion for our story to resonate with others.

The best time to begin thinking about how you would like to edit your videos is when you are creating the video content. When you create the content with editing at the front of your mind, you can envision how the final product will look and how your target audience will receive it. While creating your video content, consider the camera angles that you will use, the lighting in your bedroom, or outdoors, and your audio requirements, such as having a mic on standby. You can also make editing more convenient by splitting your video content into bite-size scenes or shots that can be edited separately (instead of editing one bulk of content and finding errors in the middle of it).

Moreover, you should consider investing in the best editing tools that you can afford. I find that quality editing tools can take an average video and turn it into a professionally designed piece of content. At the beginning of your career as an influencer, I recommend that you sample some of the free video editing software available on various smartphones and PC's. Once you start gaining a considerate number of subscribers, you can consider investing in a subscription-based editing software that will allow you to use more advanced editing tools to polish your videos. Additionally, you will need to start thinking about the equipment you plan to use to record your videos. Some influencers may prefer using professional HD cameras or camcorders, and others may prefer to use their smartphones. Nowadays, smartphones can produce the same quality images or videos that professional cameras can; therefore, I will leave this decision up to you as the influencer.

Editing YouTube videos on Your Android

An android user can create and upload their YouTube videos all on their android device. You can upload a video from your SD card and onto your channel, or create the video on your YouTube app for android. The YouTube app allows all users to edit their videos on the platform and upload them when the editing process is complete. However, influencers should use some of the awesome (and free) android video editing apps to edit their videos, which will improve the quality of their videos.

KineMasterPro Video Editor is a video editing app available on android phones where many consider it to be the only "full-featured" app for editing YouTube videos. This app includes amazing features that will help you produce professional videos. Some of these features include picture effects, adding overlays, adjusting the brightness, and trimming the videos. All of these features that are available after a simple download are free. Another free video editing app that is rated four out of five stars is Adobe Premiere Clip. This app takes away the hassle in editing videos with its simple, user-friendly interface. There are many features that users can expect when downloading this app. Some include the ability to drag and drop soundtracks into your videos and combine other clips and images to your video to turn it into one smooth video clip. Users will also have the ability to add a soundtrack accompanying their videos without losing the audio quality between video clips.

Editing YouTube videos on Your iPhone or iPad

It is no secret that Apple products are a fan favorite in shooting quality high-resolution photography and video content. However, as handy as your Apple devices may be, there are still imperfections that can only be corrected by using a video editing app. Some imperfections you may want to adjust are the consistency in lighting, trimming off unwanted portions of our video, or fixing shaky footage. Thankfully, iPhones and iPads support a multitude of video editing apps (both free and paid subscriptions), which you can search for in the App Store. However, I have picked two amazing apps that are free for you to experiment with.

The first one is one of my favorites because of the production quality produced once you have toggled with some free tools. The app I am referring to is FilmoraGo, and it is by far the most convenient video editing app on the market. It allows users to upload their videos and select one of their themes, designs, or music to accompany the finished product. Some of the spectacular features that it comes with include adding voice-overs, incorporating elements and transitions, and adding an overlay, and trim, crop, and rotate videos.

Another great iOS compatible video editing app is iMovie. iMovie is a free and comprehensive video editing tool developed by Apple. The app allows users to add titles, voice-overs, music, and photos to their videos. It also includes a variety of video templates, themes, and filters that can improve the aesthetics of any video. Videos can also be enhanced by adding your own narration and by fast-forwarding or slowing down the clip's speed. There are many editing features available on this editing software to practice your editing skills and become a pro at creating quality video footage.

The Basic Housekeeping Rules for using YouTube

A few years ago, YouTube was merely a video-sharing platform where people would go to watch funny cat videos. Even though there is still a demand for these hilarious videos, YouTube has since become known to produce diverse content. The platform has built its reputation as the second largest search engine (apart from Google) that has attracted many more viewers, collaborators, and advertisers. These consumers have decided to ditch the traditional television marketing for a more contemporary and lucrative online video-sharing market.

Becoming a successful YouTube influencer is possible because YouTube users are always willing to embrace a unique brand. This is the best time to take advantage of the many opportunities that are available to you when you grow your personal YouTube channel. To help you make a strong start in your YouTube journey, I have put together some basic rules that will guide you along the path of victory and allow your brand to be listed among the best.

The Basic Housekeeping Rules for using YouTube

- ☐ **Know your success metric.** Decide on what you aim to achieve in each phase of your channel growth. For instance, you could decide that you want more people to view your videos, or maybe you want more conversions and click-throughs. Setting a goal for what success will look like will help you create a targeted content strategy.
- ☐ **Research common keywords.** Researching keywords frequently searched for on YouTube will give you direction in creating relevant content. Therefore, it can

be easily found from a quick YouTube search and shared across multiple social media platforms.
- ☐ **Learn more about your competition.** Find out what type of content the popular YouTube influencers are posting and observe how their video content is edited, the call-to-action, and how the influencer engages with their viewers. This will help you improve the quality of your content and train yourself, while in the beginning stages, to form the same habits of high-performers.
- ☐ **Provide an in-depth video description.** Many people may overlook the importance of a video description because it seems irrelevant. However, your description box can be how some visitors find your page through SEO. For instance, a visitor may have been looking for information that you have shared in your video, and a simple keyword search of the same keywords you wrote in your video description will place your video in front of their eyes.
- ☐ **Insert a few links in your videos.** Inserting links to your other videos offers the viewer an opportunity to sample more than one of your video content. It will help you showcase the variety of topics you are able to speak on, and this will build your credibility as being a thought leader or reputable voice in your particular niche. However, make sure that you do not insert too many or allow the links to obstruct your video's viewing experience. I recommend that you add a link to your highest-performing video after you have provided the viewer with as much value as possible.

Chapter 4: How to Market Your Brand on Instagram

The concept of "influencer marketing" began on Instagram when the popular social media platform introduced us to visual storytelling. This app, which is now worth over $100 billion, offered creatives and brands a space to maximize the use of images to connect with like-minded people. Perhaps the reason why Instagram is favored by influencers more than other social networking sites is that it is easy to find and create communities on the platform, resulting in a curated experience instead of being cluttered with irrelevant content. One of the reasons why most influencers will have an Instagram account (among their list of other social media accounts) is because Instagram reigns supreme when it comes to engagement.

Indeed, Instagram makes building a personal brand a breeze because there are multiple ways of creating meaningful content. Connecting to your target audience is achievable through the use of targeted hashtags and posts. It is also easier to differentiate your brand on Instagram by using unique themes, filters, photography, and quirky content ideas. Instagram is also useful for influencer marketing because it is one of the few social media platforms that have created a lucrative environment for brand ambassadorship. It is common for users to see one of their friends promoting a new product from a local business or recommending the services of another because brands love to use Instagram for authentic product reviews, campaigns, and new releases. This is because a picture can tell a thousand words—especially when it is shared within closed communities.

Influencer marketing on Instagram is effective because an advertisement doesn't feel or look like one. Rather, the content can take on any tone, style, or message, depending on the influencer who is endorsing it and the caption associated with it. What would've sounded corny using traditional advertising is pulling at the heartstrings of the target audience and evoking a passion, longing, or desire for the product or service. Therefore, I would say that Instagram's superpower lies in the effectiveness of creating imagery to relate, connect, and empathize with the target audience. Influencers also have the opportunity to build relationships with their followers, strengthening their promotional activities and sponsored campaigns. By the time brands approach them for work opportunities, the influencers have already built a loyal community of followers who are willing to listen, engage, and act on the influencer's leadership and instruction.

Many people debate over what exactly qualifies an individual to become an Instagram influencer. While you may find many different standards or criteria online regarding this controversial topic, I will share my thoughts on how you will know once you have "made it" on Instagram. Firstly, let me start by saying an influencer is not determined by the number of followers they have because nowadays, followers may be ghost followers (fake bot profiles) or many times followers are bought. The problem with buying followers is that they do not necessarily fit into the target audience that you want to promote to—and this won't help brands when they come knocking at your door either.

I believe that the level of engagement that an individual can create on their Instagram page qualifies them as an influencer. I say this because the only proof that brands have of the influencer having some social media power is if their followers are physically engaging through comments and following the instructions laid out by the influencer. In essence, brands are looking for influencers who have firm control over their personal brand and can manage and influence their community to buy a product or view a website through clever content and messaging.

Building and Engaging with Your Instagram Community

Well-crafted Instagram posts can stir up emotions in us, and the visual impact can cause us to make personal lifestyle decisions or transformations. It can make us escape to a tropical island or imagine how it would feel like to own a new BMW. This ability to transport users to any particular place or allow them to visualize their lives enriched by new products or services is a powerful skill that all influencers will learn. To connect with your followers in such an intimate way whereby they allow you to take them on imaginary journeys is established through building a strong community.

Every influencer desires to have their own community on Instagram. An Instagram community is defined as a network made up of engaged and enthusiastic followers, potential brand partners, and other influential personal brands that support your brand. Building a community is not dependent on the number of followers you have; I have seen many successful communities built with their Instagram page having less than 10,000 followers. Instead, communities are built through people showing invested interest in your brand and helping you to push your content forward. Having viewers or hundreds of likes on a post is great; however, building a culture where your followers become fans and use every opportunity to comment and tag their friends on your posts is impressive! Below are a few strategies that will help you build a healthy community of engaged followers on Instagram.

Strategy 1: Take Time to Design Your Feed

Your Instagram page is your first opportunity to connect with new visitors. Depending on your aesthetic, visitors will decide whether your brand could potentially provide value in their lives. A beautifully themed Instagram page will also add a level of credibility to your brand. For instance, if you say that you are a wildlife photographer, visitors will expect to see images of animals in the wild or beautiful landscapes. Similarly, if you say that you are a lover of food, visitors will expect to see high-quality images of food shot at unique angles and allowing them to feel as though they were ordering it at a restaurant. Your page layout should be cohesive, maintaining the same filter, theme, colors, or typography throughout a campaign, season, or until you decide to refresh your look.

Strategy 2: Be Authentic

I believe that all humans can detect a fake from miles away. It is evident to spot one from the forced or pretentious presentation or how they emulate a well-known celebrity in their choice of content and their messages. Your followers are exposed to thousands of brands daily; however, they have never seen a brand express the way you express yours. Being authentic to who we are allows us to become vulnerable in sharing parts that make us unique. When you hold back from taking calculated risks with your content or rob your followers from understanding what your values are and what causes you support, it compromises the quality and depth of relationships that you can build. Therefore, share your grievances, fears, or excitement because truthfulness is appreciated and rewarded.

Strategy 3: Be Proactive About Creating Engagement

As much as you can produce the most appealing content deserving of quality engagement, your followers cannot read your mind or catch the subliminal messages that you have dropped in your caption. You will need to spell it out for them and guide them through the instructions that you desire for them to follow. Remember that this is your brand. At the beginning of your Instagram journey, you will need to set the expectations; eventually, they will learn how to interact with your posts and automatically complete your desired instructions. However, in the beginning, you will need to do a lot of heavy lifting. For instance, your instructions should be as clear as this: "Double-tap my picture if you agree with me" or "tag a friend who reminds you of X."

Strategy 4: Create a Sense of Belonging

Every individual loves to belong; this includes your followers too. When we are recognized for being part of a group or for our achievements, we are more likely to feel a sense of loyalty toward that organization, group, or individual. Your followers want to share the stage with you and be acknowledged every now and again for their loyalty and support. You can create a sense of belonging by creating a unique name for your fans and referring to this exclusive name when you want to thank or acknowledge them. You can also create a custom hashtag that you can put in all your captions, or feature a few of your fans on your feed. Regardless of how you do it, your followers will feel respected and appreciated by your frequent gestures fostering a sense of community and belonging.

Strategy 5: Host Competitions and Run Campaigns

Hosting a competition on your Instagram page can create excitement and a lot of buzz, I mean, who doesn't like to receive free gifts? Instagram has amazing tools that can help you run a successful competition without the hassle, leaving you to create an offer that most Instagrammers won't refuse. There are a few options available regarding the type of competition that you can run. For instance, you can run competitions that seek to collect many "likes" on a post, ones that require users to tag their friends, or answer a question, or photo challenges where users take a photo of themselves performing some function or using a product.

Guidelines for Brand Collaborations and Sponsored Posts

Instagram collaborations will assist you in effectively turning what you considered to be a skill or talent into a career through brand collaborations and sponsorships. Usually, when brands approach influencers for collaborations, they have officially reached a point where their personal brand can pay off. Indeed, the sweet incentive of collaborations is the income that it can generate. The amount of money that collaborations pay varies depending on your brand's influence and on the service that the company desires for you to do. In the beginning stages of the brand, influencers might be offered products or discounts and coupons from promoting a company's brand. Do not be dismayed by this offer because your mission in the beginning stages is to receive experience working with as many brands as you can. This way you can increase your experience level and exposure fairly quickly (this will also look impressive on your media kit).

One of the popular myths that I would like to address is the myth that you need to be a large brand or have a significant number of followers before you can approach brands or allow brands to contact you. Thanks to Instagram's updated algorithms, smaller Instagram pages can compete with larger pages and receive the attention from brands. The updated algorithm rewards pages that have a high percentage of engagement (regardless of their size). This explains why you can find photos with 5,000 likes and others with 800 likes on the Explore page. Therefore, focusing on increasing audience engagement can be a free and organic way of getting your brand noticed.

The general rule of thumb in choosing the best collaborations is to understand all that is required of you before you agree to anything. This is because there might be some hidden clauses or commitments that you are not prepared to do. One of the first steps you can take is to ask for your offer to be put in writing to have evidence of the agreed-upon terms and conditions. If the company is too small or informal to provide you with a legal document, you can create your own contract template and send it to them for electronic signage. The second step would be to ensure that all of the collaborations you agree to align with your brand.

Remember that your consistency matters, even when you think nobody is watching. The collaborations that you sign up for can either hurt or positively build your brand. It would be in your best interest to consider whether the collaboration is authentic to who you are and whether it reaffirms your value proposition. Compromising yourself in the beginning of your career is never a good thing because what you attach your name to can be found through a quick Google search by potential brand partners in the future. To help you choose the best brands to collaborate with, I would recommend that you only select brands that form a part of your niche and whose message, value offer, or style, can compliment your brand or increase your brand's value.

The Effectiveness of Using Mixed Media

I have often heard people say, "If you didn't Instagram it, it didn't happen." It is sentiments like these that show the popularity and power of Instagram in creating and sharing valuable content. Perhaps another element provided by Instagram that allows brands to easily produce interesting content is the many ways in which content can be created on the platform. Most social media platforms host content but fail to provide an in-house content generating machine similar to the one we find on Instagram. I believe that it is the ability to constantly alternate the type of content you share as an influencer that keeps your followers hungry for more. Therefore, playing around with various types of media and content will help you communicate the same message about your brand in many ways. Below are some of the amazing types of content that you can create using Instagram:

Instagram Stories

Instagram stories are a great tool to use when you have interesting daily content to share with your community, which may not necessarily be appropriate for the theme or campaign that you are promoting on your feed. Instagram stories can also be used in campaigns or collaborations to share clickable links to websites or other Instagram pages. It is important that you represent your brand in your stories because stories can draw new traffic of visitors who may be visiting your page for the first time. View your Instagram stories as your daily or weekly sales pitch to explain why your brand is unique and valuable. You can heighten your stories' visual appeal by adding music, moving graphics, behind-the-scenes videos, and quirky descriptions.

Carousel Ads

Carousel ads were first developed on Facebook's platform; however, they have become a major hit on Instagram. To simply put it, a carousel ad is a form of advertisement that allows the promoter to include a variety of images and videos into one ad format. Usually, carousel ads can show three to five images or videos in one ad unit, giving the promoter plenty of room to sell their value proposition. Influencers, in particular, can use carousel ads to tell a story about the brand that they are promoting (this can also include your own brand). You can tell a story about the various features or benefits of a product, or show unique aspects of your personal brand that will encourage Instagram users to visit your page.

IGTV

IGTV and Instagram are two separate downloadable apps (similar to Facebook Messenger and Facebook); however, they work together in uplifting the quality of content for influencers. The main purpose of IGTV is to allow users to create and share videos that are perhaps too long to post on an Instagram story (however unlike Instagram story videos, these long-form videos can stay on your channel permanently). Influencers can use IGTV to produce shareable video content on Instagram while also including meaningful "Swipe Up" call-to-actions on their video content. Some of the content that you can share through IGTV are tutorials for using products, discussing a topic or answering community questions, documenting your day, or producing your own Instagram show or series. Once you have created your IGTV video, you can always cross-promote it by sharing a link to your video on your Instagram story.

Instagram Live Videos

Instagram live videos are gaining more popularity now than ever before. The advantage of using Instagram live videos is that your video content can stream in real-time. Moreover, they provide a great opportunity for influencers and brands to communicate directly to their fans in real-time. I would encourage the use of live videos once your Instagram page has shown signs of positive engagement. In cases like this, regular live videos can boost the number of traffic that comes onto your page and increase the number of loyal followers in your community. Some of the content that you can share on an Instagram live video is behind-the-scenes footage in real-time. This may include footage taken at an event or festival that you are attending. Your live video can also show a tour around your office or home, cooking recipes in real-time, and taking the time to be transparent with your followers, sharing personal stories, or discussing a trend.

Instagram Reels

Instagram's latest add-on has a striking resemblance to TikTok. Instagram Reels are the platform's newest offering, allowing users an opportunity to record 15-second clips with Instagram's selection of music added onto them. This feature creates yet another form of media on the platform, helping content creators create fun and engaging short clips. These clips reflect on the Explore page, on Instagram Stories, as well as appearing on the new Reels tab on user profiles. On the Reels feed, users can scroll through short clips from their friends, and from popular or trending Instagram accounts. When a Reel appears on the Explore page, Instagram will notify the user and add a "Featured" tag on the bottom left corner of their video. While the Reels algorithm remains unknown at this point, the criteria of making your Reels featured is likely dependent on the originality and entertainment value of the Reels. While IGTV delivers on series-based full-length content, Reels provide high-quality informal content with a shelf life longer than twenty-four hours.

Tips to Increase Content Engagement on Instagram

Instagram reigns supreme when compared to other social media platforms regarding engagement. According to Forrester, engagement on Instagram is among the highest at a rate of 4.21% (taking into consideration like, comments, and shares from users) which is 10 times higher than Facebook's rate for engagement, 54 times higher than Pinterest's, and 84 times higher than Twitter's (Elliott, 2015). Algorithms constantly change on social media platforms, and Instagram is not an exception to this. This means that sooner or later, influencers will need to learn how to boost their engagement, particularly when Instagram changes its algorithm or new competitors in the market, such as TikTok, begin to steal its limelight and reduce Instagram's engagement rate. Therefore, below are some tips that I have compiled for you, which will help you maximize your ability to make your content actionable.

Tips to Increase Content Engagement on Instagram

1. Post regularly (at least one or two posts a day).
2. Provide creative visuals that challenge content that is already available to the public.
3. Select the most appropriate, niche-specific hashtags, avoid generic hashtags, and don't place too many hashtags that can make your page seem unprofessional.
4. Create your own branded hashtag that is short but catchy.
5. Consider using subtitles on your Instagram videos to help you deliver your message while also communicating through the visual content.
6. Be creative when formatting your Instagram videos, taking advantage of all of the many cool AR filters, effects, and overlays available.
7. Have a plan to drive your Instagram traffic to another social media platform or your blog or website.
8. Be clear in your call-to-actions by making simple sentences that provide a single direction.
9. Track the performance of your content and learn the patterns of how your audience receives your content. Make the necessary changes to your content strategy if needs be.
10. Find new and interesting ways of sharing your brand message. Perhaps you can explore other hobbies or interests that align with your brand, or collaborate with other Instagram influencers that complement your brand's style and voice.

Chapter 5: How to Market Your Brand on Facebook

Facebook is the largest social media platform where most social media users were first introduced to a mega community of like-minded people (I am yet to find a person who has never opened a Facebook account). This social media platform, which has over 2.6 billion monthly users across the world (Noyes, 2019), was one of the first platforms to expose people to content marketing. It made it easy for people to stay in touch with relatives and friends through the liking and sharing of videos, status updates, and images. The bigger the Facebook community grew, the more brands started to join the platform and promote their products and services. Through Facebook ads, brands were now able to advertise their products between news feeds, create unique sponsored videos, effectively run campaigns and hashtags and content that could be linked or directed to another website or blog.

Over the past few years, Facebook has made some updates to its social media site that have indirectly created an opportunity for influencers to help brands promote their products. At some point or another, every social media platform will update their algorithm, which is a way for the platform to organize content on user feeds by filtering content into what is relevant for the user to see and what is not. One of the many changes to the algorithm that the social media site has recently made is to limit the number of organic company posts and advertisements on users' feeds. This move was carried out because branded posts were seen—by the larger Facebook community—as a distraction and compromising on the personal moments that could be shared between friends or family.

Limiting organic company posts did not necessarily mean that companies would be barred from posting about their products or services. However, it meant that when companies would attempt to promote their products or services on Facebook organically, they would not receive the quality of engagement or traffic that they would hope for (unless, of course, they were to promote their post with Facebook Ads). In essence, the only strategic way for any company or professional brand to get its name out on Facebook is through paying the platform for advertising space. This offer may still be appealing for some companies; however, those whose brands are built on having an authentic connection with communities of people may prefer leveraging on an influencer's Facebook following and continue to promote their brand "organically.

Now more than ever before, companies are reaching out to influencers to help them promote or increase awareness of their brands on their news feed. These companies understand that using an influencer is more valuable than paying for advertising space. One of the benefits that an influencer can provide—which a paid Facebook Ad cannot—is to create meaningful connections with the target audience. In 2018 when the Founder and CEO of Facebook, Mark Zuckerberg, announced an update of the site's algorithm, he stated that the new direction that Facebook would take prioritized active engagement and connections with friends on Facebook instead of users passively consuming marketing content. We already know that influencer brands centers around active engagement and that their content elicits discussions and reactions. Therefore, the types of exposure and meaningful engagement that influencers can offer companies and other brands are far more valuable than paid ads.

The truth is that influencers are valuable for brand promotions in this new era of Facebook because they naturally have an authentic appeal that brands struggle to establish perhaps due to their bottom-line motives being so apparent in their marketing material. Moreover, the type of influencers we are seeing receive this amazing opportunity are micro-influencers who have a few thousand followers and are fairly new. Micro-influencers can offer brands more value because their Facebook accounts are still personal accounts and not businesses. In 2017, Facebook began a drive to push many larger influencers to convert their accounts from "public figure" to a Facebook page (which establishes the influencer as a business). When larger influencers convert to a Facebook business page, they have the same limits imposed on their account as normal companies do. Therefore, receiving the desired engagement on promoted content becomes impossible unless the content is sponsored through Facebook Ads.

Thus, I encourage many influencers, especially micro-influencers, to invest in a Facebook account and grow it organically, ensuring they are building a community of like-minded people who can become an appropriate target audience for brands. Facebook users are more likely to listen to an influencer than a brand because of how the content can sound and feel more authentic when shared by a peer. As Facebook shifts toward an emphasis on building connections, influencers need to take time in building a strong community of followers who can eventually push an influencer's promoted content forward and thus helping brands receive the kind of engagement that they truly desire.

Creating Shareable Content on Facebook

In the past few years, we have seen social media platforms reconfigure their algorithms. This has made it difficult for organic content to receive the attention and engagement that it deserves. I find that the importance of learning how to create shareable content has become significant, particularly in helping influencers grow their accounts on platforms such as Facebook. Nowadays, successful content strategies will focus on finding ways to stand out and differentiate the influencer's brand from the sea of other personal brands vying for the same spotlight.

In today's social media climate, only brands that focus on releasing exceptional content will stand out. It is no longer suitable for brands to post content fillers or unnecessary fluff that does not add value to the brand's message or objectives. The goal for any influencer should be to create content that inspires followers to like and share the post or video, with or without the algorithm's help. In other words, your content should always seek to provide value for your followers to encourage organic engagement. Below are some amazing tips for creating shareable content that will help you receive the kind of engagement you desire.

1. Do Research on Your Competitors

The best way to learn about the type of content your target audience enjoys is to find out what your competitors are sharing and how they are marketing their content. Sharing popular content will guarantee a few visitors every week to your page, allowing you to convert them into followers. To successfully spy on your competitors and learn from their content strategies, you will need to follow a few steps. Firstly, make a list of five of your competitors who are in the same niche and have a similar target audience. Locate their Facebook pages and browse through 6 months worth of content. Indeed, your fingers will become numb from the scrolling; however, pay attention to the various types of content that these competitors share and compare it with the content that you are currently sharing.

Notice the types of content that have received a high engagement rate from their followers and start picking up patterns in these high-performing content pieces. Perhaps the post performed well because of the imagery, caption, or call-to-action. It is also important to notice the types of content that did not perform so well and received barely any engagement or no engagement at all. Therefore, use their top-performing posts as an inspiration to guide your own content creation, and ensure that your content supersedes that of your competitors.

2. Speak Your Audience's Language

The role of an influencer is to be a mouthpiece for a broad community of individuals. Influencers need to understand the audience they seek to represent if they want to be a mouthpiece for them. In other words, the content shared must be relevant to the lived experiences of the target audience and, in some way, affirm their opinions, beliefs, interests, and ideas. This will encourage them to share the influencer's content because the post reaffirms what they are already sharing about themselves and their perspective on life. Thus, influencers must ensure that they have conducted a comprehensive target market analysis, gaining an understanding of their demographic, their interests, and what they truly care about.

3. Create Useful Content

Social media users—regardless of the type of social media platform—are more likely to share content that carries value. As I have mentioned earlier in the book, every human being has a brand, and this is true for every social media user. Perhaps their brand is not as influential as the influencers; however, you will find that users will only share content that is useful in the context of their brand. For instance, it is rare to find a young adult who has never had any children share a post about stretchy baby diapers. Instead, you would find posts useful to their life stage and interests, such as makeup tutorials or reviews on the latest sports cars. Sharing useful content also implies that the type of content an influencer posts is suitable to their brand's niche and makes their page look cohesive and targeted to a specific consumer.

4. Create Your Content Around Trends

Sometimes it may be tough to create unique content, especially on days when your creativity seems stifled. One great trick to use regularly is to create content that is inspired by a trending topic in your particular niche. It's worth repeating that your content should still be brand-specific, even though you are creating content from a trend. For instance, if you have a brand focused on cooking delicious classical recipes, you could create special content by releasing a themed recipe for every public holiday, festival, or celebration. A great way to find current trends is to conduct a quick search for them on Google Trends that releases a list of popular trends every day. Remember to pick trends related to your brand or niche so that your content can remain cohesive.

5. Inspire Your Followers

Another powerful way to encourage your followers to share your content is to inspire them. This could be done through an inspirational quote, a short motivational video, or an animated graphic that can invoke positive emotions. Inspirational content is popular among most social media platforms. This is because it can transform the way people perceive their capabilities. It can lift a person's mood if they were having a bad day or remind them of their awesomeness. Inspirational content further creates a favorable image of the influencer's brand. The brand is relatable and down to earth, which will ultimately attract many visitors to the influencer's page.

Strategies for SEO

Effective use of social media allows brands and influencers to establish an open line of communication with their customers or followers. Social media platforms are used to help these brands and influencers create emotional connections with their audience. This kind of connection increases audience engagement, which will have a powerful indirect effect on the brand or influencer's organic search results on Internet search engines. In other words, the brand or influencer's activities on social media platforms such as Facebook can help the company or personality effectively boost their Search Engine Optimization (SEO). This would allow for their content and other brand assets to rank high on popular search engines.

Influencers desire to have their personal brand appear in search engine results pages because this will allow them to gain as much brand exposure as possible. Furthermore, when potential clients search for the influencer's brand online, they will gage the influencer's brand reputation by assessing how high the brand ranks on search results. If you take the time to search for a branded keyword, you will notice how many social media profiles suddenly appear. When most consumers research a particular company, they will often explore their social media profiles first before exploring their websites. Ideally, influencers will want most of their social media profiles to appear on results pages for audiences to have full access to their brand. Below are 10 strategies that will help you optimize your Facebook page to rank high on search engine sites.

Strategy 1: Picking the Best Name

Having a distinct and memorable name will make searching for your brand a breeze. Many influencers choose generic names that do not differentiate their brand enough in their particular niche or choose names inappropriate for the platform. Facebook is also strict when it comes to brands using names with too many branded keywords that appear to be one fat marketing sales pitch. I recommend that influencers avoid using any marketing reference, catch-phrases or slogans in their name, or any other word manipulation like: tHe_liTTle_BIG_cOOk

Strategy 2: Use Brand-specific Keywords

Keywords are a powerful tool to use in optimizing your Facebook page. The rule is to use as many relevant keywords on your page descriptions and within your content and captions. The emphasis here should be placed on the word *relevant* because using generic keywords that are trending online will make your page seem fraudulent or spammy (this would cause the adverse effects and sink your Google ranking). Another tip is to ensure that your Facebook keywords are specific to your objectives for targeting a Facebook audience.

When influencers use the same keywords on all of their social media platforms, they miss out on an opportunity to create content specific to the crowd found in that particular social media platform. For instance, Facebook is primarily useful for creating brand awareness and brand promotions; therefore, the best keywords to use on the platform would focus on highlighting the products or services that you or the company that you represent offers. The best spots on your Facebook page to insert these keywords would be in the page title, page headline, about and description section, post captions, status updates, and when you are tagging or linking other websites.

Strategy 3: Use a Custom URL

Using a custom and branded Facebook URL can significantly boost your SEO efforts because it allows for members of your audience to remember how to access your page and easily recommend your Facebook page to others. A memorable custom Facebook URL is always simple and relevant to the brand; typically, the URL would simply include the brand name. Facebook requires for business pages to have at least 25 likes before they can create a branded Facebook URL. This minor requirement is worth the investment of a custom URL, which will allow your brand to gain credibility online.

Strategy 4: Keep Your Contact Information Updated

It is understandable how brands sometimes forget to update their contact details from when they set up their Facebook accounts and again when some of their details change. However, having outdated contact information makes reaching the brand difficult. Traditional contact details play an important role in making the influencer more accessible online and helping potential clients make formal contact with you. I would say that sharing up-to-date contact details is the final and most valuable call-to-action that will make all of the influencer's marketing efforts worthwhile. The more personal contact information you include, the more visibility you will achieve on search engine result pages. For instance, adding your office address will generate Google maps to help clients locate you, and including your website URL will allow audiences to find more of your content online.

Strategy 5: Create Powerful CTA's

As effective as our content may be in driving traffic to our blogs or websites, posts without call-to-actions perform poorly compared to those that included clear and actionable instructions. People love to be led because it helps them create decisions within a shorter time than if they had to judge or make decisions on their own. Influencers need to be proactive in guiding their community of Facebook friends and interpreting the content in the manner in which the influencer desires it to come across. Call-to-actions will help your fans engage with your brand in the most meaningful way possible. When creating call-to-actions, remember to use action words that request an action to follow. You can use action words such as: sign up, like, share, comment, tag, watch, or download.

How to Use Facebook Ads to Boost Sales and Traffic

Facebook advertising is one of the surest ways of connecting and engaging with your audience on Facebook. It also exposes the influencer's brand to the largest community of social media users on the Internet. In other words, the effective use of advertising on Facebook will give the influencer the much-needed brand recognition that they desire. Another reason why Facebook Ads are becoming more and more useful is due to the ever-changing Facebook algorithm, which has made it difficult for brands to connect with their audience organically. In essence, Facebook has created an environment where brands need to pay for exposure and engagement instead of receiving it for free.

Those who have the marketing budget to promote their brands with Facebook Ads can increase their chances of connecting with like-minded individuals and building a curated community. This is done by using the platform's targeting features, which allows the advertiser to reach a particular audience that will be more receptive to the brand and more likely to benefit from the sponsored products and services. The wide variety of adverts allows advertisers to communicate their brand message through strategic campaigns that will give them the best results. Below is a list of the types of adverts that Facebook offers for brand promotions:

1. **Image Ads**

Image adverts are a great way of introducing your brand to your chosen target audience. They are also the simplest form of an advert to set up; influencers can create an image advert with just a few clicks by promoting their existing image post from their Facebook page.

2. **Video Ads**

Video adverts are becoming popular on social media news feeds because of how they can boost their audience engagement rate. Video adverts on Facebook can be positioned within public news feeds or in Facebook stories. This advertising format is useful for showing audiences how a product functions (this could be done through tutorials, slideshows, or demonstrations).

3. **Carousel Ads**

Carousel adverts on Facebook allow the advertiser to arrange up to 10 images or videos advertising the brand or sponsored products and services in one marketing presentation. Carousel adverts are typically used to highlight the benefits of using a particular product or service, or at times they are creatively arranged together to form one panorama image.

4. Lead Ads

Lead adverts are a great tool to use when you require members of your target audience to share their contact information with you. While this advertising format is only available on mobile devices, it is still useful in helping influencers build their mailing lists by encouraging audiences to sign up for their newsletters, limited trials, visit their profile, or directly message them for more information.

5. Messenger Ads

Another fantastic type of Facebook advertising format available to advertisers is the messenger advert, which places all sponsored adverts directly on Facebook Messenger. This advertising strategy allows influencers to reach some of the 1.3 billion Facebook users who actively engage in Messenger every month. Another great feature about messenger adverts is that they include a call-to-action button, which when followed, creates a new Messenger conversation where the user can start a conversation with the influencer about the sponsored product or service.

The main criterion for influencers to become eligible for advertising on Facebook is to switch to a Facebook business account. Facebook business accounts will provide influencers with all of the advertising and analytical tools needed to grow their Facebook page and connect with the desired audience. However, as I have mentioned above, creating a business account means that the influencer is treated like a business owner, making organic reach seemingly impossible. Therefore, influencers who are considering switching from a personal account to a business account should be willing to invest a reasonable budget toward promoting their Facebook content.

Once you have created your Facebook business account, you can head over to the Facebook Ads Manager tab to create all of your Facebook campaigns. Below is a step-by-step guide in creating a simple Facebook campaign:

Step 1: Choose Specific Objectives

The first step requires you to decide on the specific objective you hope to achieve with your single post. This does not necessarily need to be the same as your overall brand objective. Instead, it should target how you want audience members to react from your unique piece of content. Currently, Facebook offers 11 marketing objectives, which have a different purpose and goal for promoting your brand. These objectives range from raising awareness of the brand to helping audiences purchase products from third-party e-commerce stores.

Step 2: Name Your Campaign

Now that you have set your campaign objectives, you can name your campaign and choose whether you want to create an A/B split test (which will compare the performance of two or more campaigns alongside each other). If your objective were to promote your Facebook page, you would also have an opportunity to select which Facebook page you want to promote.

Step 3: Create a Target Audience

Now you can start building your target audience. You will find two options; you can either create an audience from the Facebook friends who are already following you or create a custom audience you will create from choosing a list of characteristics, demographics, and interests. I believe that the more detailed your targeting is, the greater your chances of receiving an ROI and reaching the people you desire to connect to.

Step 4: Decide on Your Advert Placement

Now that you have created a target audience, you can choose where you would like your advert positioned on Facebook's platform. For those influencers who are new to Facebook Ads, you can start by selecting automatic placements that will allow Facebook to decide on the best area to place your advert, including placement on Instagram and Messenger. Once you are more experienced in creating campaigns, you can select where you want to put the ads on your own, choosing between feeds, stories, in-article, other social media apps such as Instagram, in-videos, or on Messenger.

Step 5: Decide on a Budget and Schedule

The final and crucial step is to decide on how much money you wish to spend on your campaign. Here you will be presented with two more options. You can decide on a daily budget dedicated to promoting your advert, or you can choose to promote it indefinitely (this works well when your campaign objective is to create awareness of your Facebook page). In this step, you will also decide on the start and end date of your campaign, or whether you prefer to schedule it for a later date. It is important to note that schedules can only be set for lifetime campaigns, which run indefinitely. Once you have selected on a budget and a date, you will see an estimate of the size of the audience that you can potentially attract with your campaign. Audience size is also dependent on the budget you are willing to spend; increasing your budget will also extend your audience reach.

How to Create a Look-alike Audience

Facebook is always hard at work, ensuring that the Facebook Ads system is optimized to serve the needs of brands. One of the new developments introduced has optimized targeting individuals who are as closely related to the brand's target audience. This is widely known as Facebook's look-alike audience, and it is now available as an option on new campaigns. In simple terms, a look-alike audience allows brands more quality leads on Facebook. It seeks to connect brands with people who share more common traits and interests with the brand by using optimizations that have assisted the brand in the past.

In essence, this means that brands can now filter through audiences more thoroughly and reach members of the Facebook community who share the same location, age, interests, and gender with the brand's current customers. This kind of targeted data is collected through behavior patterns of Facebook users and the type of regular visitors that the brand's Facebook page receives. Look-alike audiences originate from the pixels that the brand previously set on their website or their custom audience. Sometimes, the brand may prefer to base their look-alike audience on the kind of visitors they receive on their page, blogs, or from a customer lead list that the brand has directly uploaded on Facebook.

I would say that look-alike audiences are useful to brands that desire to market to a precise group of people to maximize their ROI and boost their chances of converting visitors into loyal fans or customers. A look-alike audience is effective when used in conjunction with clear campaign objectives that will improve the campaign's overall performance and success. The minimum number of people you can reach through a look-alike audience is 100; however, you can create up to 500 look-alike audiences from a generic audience. It is also worth noting that the existing members of your Facebook community (your Facebook friends) will not feature in your look-alike audiences. Your existing community forms a unique audience on its own, which you must select should you wish to market your content to them.

Chapter 6: How to Market Your Brand on Pinterest

Pinterest is not merely an image-sharing social media platform. Since its launch in 2010, Pinterest has proven to be a contender among the largest social networking websites, boasting 322 million active monthly users (Cover, 2019). Over the years, Pinterest has grown to become a useful digital marketing tool, helping brands share their content and direct the masses to third party websites such as blogs, websites, or other social media platforms. I would describe Pinterest as being a virtual bulletin board that allows brands to share visual inspiration in various lifestyle categories. Users can either follow the links inserted in the image captions or *pin* visual inspiration on custom boards they have created.

Pinterest's main value is to provide a positive space where users can find inspiration on their future purchases, visions boards, and ideas for fun lifestyle hobbies, fashion, beauty, renovations, interior design, DIY projects, or delicious recipes. While Facebook offers a great platform for sharing promotional content, Pinterest is a platform where brands and influencers share their personality, beliefs, values, philosophies, and personal style. Even though brands do successfully market their products or services on Pinterest, the tone and style of the content are less of a sales pitch and more about sharing a lifestyle with the targeted audience.

There are three ways in which brands and influencers can effectively capitalize on Pinterest to connect and engage with their target audience. Firstly, brands and influencers can benefit from Pinterest by gathering inspiration and style ideas. Many people (including brands) will scroll through Pinterest to research current trends in various lifestyle categories. This research is important for brands because it provides them with an indication of what the brand's target audience enjoys, trending products, and general interests and hobbies of their desired customer.

Other lifestyle brands will collect ideas on Pinterest by creating boards with images that reaffirm the brand's vision, interests, and style. For instance, an influencer who is a beauty blogger can capitalize on Pinterest by creating various boards focused on beauty inspiration, which will help members of their target audience learn how to apply makeup or use skincare products creatively. By sharing beauty inspiration, the influencer would be establishing themselves as a credible voice online, encouraging users to follow their page for more tips and advice.

The second way in which brands and influencers can capitalize on Pinterest is when they seek to push out content. Pinterest's platform facilitates the sharing of ideas and interests between community members, thereby allowing branded content to be easily found and pinned or shared with others. Pinterest will also help brands with their marketing efforts by allowing them to customize their URLS, provide them with a 200 character description box on their profiles, and enable brands to share links to third party websites. An ideal scenario for any brand is for a Pinterest user to follow their custom boards. Following a brand's board shows interest in the content that is pinned. This public display of interest would compel brands to post frequently and consistently to form relationships with users and create a Pinterest community.

The third benefit that Pinterest provides to brands and influencers is the ability to share more information about their product or service that users would not find on the brand's website, social media accounts, or blog. Supplementary information can be shared through video content with a link directing traffic to a website or blog or through charts and infographics that explain concepts, features, and benefits related to an industry or specific niche. Brands may also use Pinterest to share their website or blog content and help their audience stay updated on new content releases. Cross-promotional activities such as these will also help the brand attract new visitors to their website, blog, or other social media accounts.

However, the main goal that a brand or influencer should strive for on Pinterest is to make their content go viral. This is not an impossible task, especially when you have created visually appealing and engaging content. Viral content is pinned on Pinterest's opular page and gains a lot of viewership and click-throughs from the millions of active users that browse through the platform's content every day. On Pinterest's popular page, you can expect to find a variety of lifestyle images, tips, advice, project inspiration, and find new and niche brands. Most of the pins on this page are useful and therefore encourage users to share them easily. I intend to show you how your content can also be listed among the brands and individuals on Pinterest's popular page and gain organic traffic flowing to your profile and to any other online location you seek to direct traffic to.

Using Pinterest to Drive Traffic to Your Brand

There is a common misconception that Pinterest only caters to mommy bloggers, fashion gurus, or foodies. The truth is that this social media platform is technically more of a visual search engine than a social networking website. Bloggers have been driving traffic from Pinterest to their blog sites for years. Even the numbers prove to us that there must be some merit in Pinterest's ability to mobilize communities of people to support brands. For instance, studies find that a singular pin can lead to up to twopage visits and up to six-page views (Cain, 2020).

Furthermore, we have seen brands like Apple, Wal-Mart, and Lowe's implement successful digital marketing strategies using Pinterest to emphasize their brand's story. Perhaps part of the success that these brands have experienced on Pinterest is due to the longer lifespan of a pin than content shared on other social media platforms. For instance, it is found that a singular pin has a lifespan of one week, whereas content shared on Facebook has a lifespan of 90 minutes (Cain, 2020).

This shows us that any brand can achieve success through marketing on Pinterest, regardless of whether it is a blogger or a company in the technological or marketing industry. Even though this platform has not always been the first choice for SEO marketers or commercial brands, it is still one of the most dynamic and affordable tools for content marketing. There are many ways in which you can use Pinterest to drive its community members to your website or blog. Below are some tips that you can start implementing today, which will make Pinterest one of your favorite content marketing tools to increase your following and attract potential clients online.

Tip 1: Register for a Pinterest Business Account

To maximize the features available on Pinterest, you will have to open a free business account on the platform or switch your existing account to a business one. This is important because with a business account comes analytical tools that will guide your content marketing activities and indicate your pins' performance. Understanding how your pin is performing is crucial because it will give you the chance to improve your content or continue pinning similar kinds of content. Switching to a business account will also allow you to apply for Rich Pins, which are pins that include a lot more information in them than regular pins. Rich Pins are available in various content types that promote a specific genre, including, articles, movies, apps, recipes, products, and places. A business user can also add real-time pricing and a direct link to purchase the product or service on a third party website.

Tip 2: Pay Attention to Your Copy Description

Each pin will have a description or caption beneath it that will tell the reader more about the pin. Generally, bloggers will add their blog title and a short description of the article. However, to gain the necessary attention, you need to put in more effort than that. For instance, you need to make sure that the description is useful and offers the reader some kind of value. Moreover, the description should be detailed while also interesting to read. Having long, drawn-out descriptions will not entice a reader to click-through to your YouTube account or website; a lack of emotive or positive words will make your content seem common or not worth the effort of discovering more information. Lastly, a great description will have a clear call-to-action that will guide the reader on the next best decision to make. Ensure that the call-to-action includes actionable words such as "check out" or "read more."

Tip 3: Timing Is Important

Your efforts to drive traffic to your brand must involve timing your content and only pinning in the most opportune times. The fact is that hundreds of pins are uploaded on Pinterest every hour of the day; however, not every hour is the best time for you to share your content. Remember that your goal should be to generate viral content, and hence you will need to release content when the Pinterest community is most engaged. However, to go viral, we must first have a good track record of pinning consistently so that Pinterest can see our page activity and know that we are actively engaging. Therefore, I recommend that you should start by pinning continuously for 30 days. These initial pins must be of high quality and provide as much information about your brand as possible.

After a month of tracking your content, you can use a powerful app known as Tailwind, which is a favorite among pinners for scheduling pins on Pinterest. It can save your desired time and date you want to release your pin on and effectively pin it on time, even when you are not online. Tailwind will also track your pins' performance and provide you with major trends that are currently occurring on Pinterest. When scheduling your pins on Tailwind, you should always pick the best times and days to post your pins on Pinterest. Saturday evenings are known to be the best times to post on Pinterest, with popular times being 8 p.m. to 11 p.m. and 2 a.m. to 4 a.m.

Tip 4: Create Pin-worthy Content

The fascination with Pinterest is due to the quality of the images users post that inspires an emotive reaction from the readers. It is as if the image speaks to the reader's thoughts, dreams, and ambitions, and thus, the image becomes a part of their personal board, symbolizing the connectedness to the content's message. By creating pin-worthy content, you will gain more followers as users desire to see more of your content and use it for their own inspiration. Creating engaging images on Pinterest comes with a few requirements. Firstly, the images need to be the right size. One of the more obvious tips is always to share vertical images because most of the users on Pinterest access the app on mobile devices, making taller (instead of wider) images appear better.

Typically, the perfect image would have an aspect ratio of 2:3 or 4:5, depending on your preference. The general rule of thumb is to go as long as you can (without compromising the quality of the message or image). The longer the image is, the more space it consumes on your feed and therefore making it unmissable. Secondly, your images need to be aesthetically beautiful. You would be surprised by what kind of images users tend to prefer. Firstly it may be shocking to read, but images without a human face tend to receive 23% more re-pins than images with a human face. This is because users prefer to pin objects, information, or arrangements instead of a portrait of somebody. Furthermore, add as much color as you can, incorporate as much light as possible, and choose a background that adds depth to your overall image.

Lastly, it is important to include text in your image if you desire direct traffic to your website or blog. Text is not only beneficial to make the image appear more professional, it also provides a quick summary of what the topic or message of your pin focuses on. This will help users decide within a glance whether they are interested in viewing the pin and proceeding with the written call-to-action. Nowadays, there is a lot of free software, which allows you to edit your images and add text to them. Two of my favorites would have to be Canva and PicMonkey. However, if you are looking to create more professional images and thus require more editing tools, it would be a great investment to purchase Adobe Photoshop and make your images stand out. Adobe Photoshop has an affordable monthly subscription for beginners, and they also provide many video tutorials to teach beginners how to edit images like a pro.

Tip 5: Consider Joining a Pinterest Group Board

A Pinterest Group Board is a board where a community of members can simultaneously use to pin their favorite content. Successful group boards play a significant role in helping brands and influencers increase the traction of their content and generate traffic on their profiles. Group boards have become popular over time, and the constant flow of traffic on them can truly help a brand gain much-needed exposure. The goal for making a group board work to your favor is to commit to posting regularly on the board.

When you post frequently, members of the group board will become more familiar with your brand, style, and message, and they might be interested in viewing more of your content on your profile. You can find a list of group boards on PinGroupie by running a quick keyword search and seeing which boards come up. Once you have found a group board, you would need to locate it on Pinterest and follow any instructions on joining the community. Perhaps you will need to contact the creator of the board, or you may need to complete a request form. Either way, it is always best to be courteous of the group's rules and conditions for posting.

The Anatomy of a Successful Pin

People flock to Pinterest in their numbers to view beautiful and inspirational photography. For many people, the experience on Pinterest is more about viewing other creators' images than posting their own. It should not be a shock then when we hear of research stating that 80% of the pins we see on our feeds are re-pins and not original content (Fitzpatrick, 2019). This is good news for brands and influencers because it means that the Pinterest community is not overly-saturated with content that looks the same. When done right, your pin can create a buzz and inspire many to feel or act favorably.

It is understandably a daunting moment when you realize that the bar is set high to produce your meaningful content and post it on Pinterest. However, there are many benefits of using as much original content as you can on your boards instead of relying predominantly on re-pins. Firstly, original content will help you build your brand in ways that re-pins can't. It will help you communicate your unique value proposition and show the audience what your boards offer that they will not find on other boards. Original content can also offer new information to your audience that they have not found in circulation. New information inevitably makes your boards more desirable, especially for avid Pinterest users who are all too familiar with the kind of content that flows through feeds. Now that you have understood the benefits of posting your original content on Pinterest, we need to discuss the factors that make a successful pin.

1. **Add Some Inspiration**

Can we even call a pin a pin if it does not inspire users? I certainly don't think so. The advantage of using imagery or video as one of your main types of content is how these mediums tell stories. Thus, a successful pin will tell a story, and it will certainly be an inspiring one that causes an emotional resonance with those who view it. It is also good to remember that Pinterest also acts as a kind of wish list in the sense that users will pin content they desire to purchase or manifest in the future. Therefore, your pins must incite some kind of desire or longing for them to be shareable. In other words, your content strategy objective for Pinterest would involve tapping into your audience's hopes and dreams and positioning your brand as one of the contributors to achieving these hopes and dreams.

2. **Create a Theme and Stick With It**

The benefit of posting your original content on Pinterest is that you can share your brand with others. This means that your content can be branded or have a consistent color scheme, theme, style, or message. Creating beautifully branded content would involve adding the same logo or brand symbol to every image or video to make your content recognizable. It would also help to stick to the same color palette and use a maximum of three colors consistently in your content. In the beginning, you can explore the kind of images that fit your brand and use the analytics gathered from your pins to decide on particular photos that you will continue to post regularly. If you decide on using images that are not yours, I recommend that you search for free images on royalty-free websites such as Unsplash, Pixabay, Pexels, or Librestock, which will give you amazing quality and ensure that you are not using creators' photographs illegally.

3. Optimize Your Content

Pinterest, like all of the other social media platforms, has its own algorithm. This means that the more your images follow this algorithm, the higher the possibility of them performing well. One way to increase your images' exposure is to optimize your descriptions by adding popular keywords. When users search Pinterest's search engine, they will punch in keywords looking for particular images. This means that your target audience will typically punch in keywords related to your specific niche. Therefore, industry-related keywords are important to place in your description, image caption, and the articles or videos that you are sharing.

4. Highlight the Strengths of Your Brand

Do not be afraid to communicate your authentic brand through your content. The more brand-specific your content is, the more engagement you are likely to receive. This is because there are so many categories and subcategories on Pinterest that you will probably find an image for any search you are looking for. You can even be color or style specific and still find hundreds of images related to your search. Therefore, differentiating your content from the rest will work in your favor. One way to differentiate yourself is to place your product or service as the focal point in the image. You can also include your logo or other branded symbols, which will help you stand out. Moreover, do not hesitate to add a call-to-action. This will indicate that there is more to be learned and shared with the viewer from accessing your profile.

5. Your Smartphone Is Your Friend

Even though it is the convenient and hassle-free solution to use royalty-free images from websites like Unsplash, it can sometimes backfire on your brand primarily because royalty-free images are most likely distributed frequently on Pinterest. This means that you are less likely to receive quality engagement when you use these images, and it may compromise on the credibility of your brand. Your smartphone can be a great device to use when seeking to recreate the same high-quality imagery you regularly find on image websites. The technology installed on smartphones has made these thin devices fit for operating professional functions such as taking professional photographs that would have otherwise been shot on a camera. When taking photos on your smartphone, pay attention to the lighting, the shadows created, and the angles your object is shot in. You can also play around with the filters used on your image, which can help make a normal image pop on an already color-saturated feed.

A Complete Pinterest Strategy for Influencers

When deciding to use Pinterest as one of your social media platforms in growing your personal brand, a great question to ask yourself before you start pushing out content is—what goal do I hope to achieve on Pinterest? For some influencers, their initial response to this question would be that they desire to get more followers on their profile. This kind of response is expected because we are bombarded with articles and blog posts telling us that the greater the number of followers an influencer has, the greater their influence. While gaining followers may prove to be somewhat useful on platforms like Instagram and Facebook, it will not necessarily work on Pinterest. This is because, above being a social media platform, Pinterest is a visual search engine where users search for images that they want to see or find products that they want to buy with a simple click-through on a pin.

Therefore, on this visual search engine, more followers will not necessarily provide the engagement that you hope for with your posts. A more appropriate goal would be to create the kind of quality content that will encourage viewers to click on your links and visit your blogs, websites, or other social media platforms. With this goal in mind, your strategy would not be to gain more followers, but you would seek to optimize your keywords, create useful hashtags, and make your images stand out.

You would start to look at the number of page visits, the number of subscribers if you had a mailing list, or the traffic flow from Pinterest onto your e-commerce store. Your goals of optimizing your content, increasing your engagement rate, and converting site visitors into purchasing customers would help you create a meaningful Pinterest strategy. Below are some of the factors that would create a complete and actionable Pinterest strategy.

- ☐ **Think like your fan.** Produce content with your ideal fan in mind. This should translate in the times you decide to post, the types of images you believe that your ideal fan desires to see, and information that you believe your ideal fan would search for.
- ☐ **Create content with your objectives in mind.** When creating campaigns on Pinterest, always consider your objectives for every piece of content you post. This will help you stay consistent with your intentions and maintain a consistent message that will be shared continuously.
- ☐ **Treat Pinterest as if it were a search engine.** Ask yourself the question: if my target audience were searching for information on Google, how would they find me? This question will help you create optimized content that focuses on using commonly searched keywords or phrases on Pinterest. A quick way to find

common keywords is to scroll to the Pinterest search bar and see all of the suggested keywords that come up when you start typing a word or phrase.
- **Continuously track the performance of your content.** It is important to detect whether a piece of content is gaining the traction you desire very early on. This will give you an indication of whether your content strategy is effective or not. It will also allow newer business accounts to test various types of content and how they perform, before deciding on the most successful posts to continue sharing.
- **Start with organic pinning before opting for paid advertising.** I would recommend those influencers who are new to Pinterest, to begin sharing their content organically (without the use of Pinterest's paid advertising). Organic pinning will help newer influencers understand the kind of audience that navigate to their page and the kind of content that this audience enjoys. This information can be used by the influencer to make the necessary adjustments to their content strategy or perhaps add necessary improvements to their existing strategy. Once you are more comfortable with the traffic coming onto your page and the kind of content that these visitors are looking for, you can proceed to promote your pins.

Chapter 7: How to Market Your Brand on TikTok

Before the popularity of TikTok, there was a viral app known as Musical.ly, which offered short-form video streaming of approximately 15 seconds a video. Musical.ly offered its young audience a vast number of musical renditions and dialogue snippets, which they could lip-sync and create entertaining or silly content. The app acquired around 100 million active users by August 2018 before it was bought by a China-based company known as ByteDance. This acquisition brought along with it a name change, turning Musical.ly into the fastest-growing social media platform we know today as TikTok.

TikTok's model is similar to the one Musical.ly was founded on; it allows users to share short-form videos that are 15 seconds long. The big difference between the two apps, however, is seen in how TikTok allows for its users to do more than just lip-sync. TikTok users have access to a variety of sounds or song snippets, special effects, and filters that may be edited into videos and also having the benefit of uploading a video created on a user's smartphone. Recently, TikTok added yet another feature, which allows users to record their reactions to other videos shared on the site. Therefore, if I were to summarize the value that TikTok offers its audience, I would say that it is a video-sharing social networking app that allows its users to create video content and share it with a public community of members.

One of the key strategies implemented by the platform that boasts 800 million active users each month, emphasized local content as a driving force to gain as many users as possible. The app aims to create smaller communities of users in each country across the world. Some of the ways that it has done this is through promoting local hashtags and tracking local trending videos. Moreover, TikTok has invested a lot of capital in partnering with celebrities across various regions as part of its geographical expansion strategy. These celebrities have endorsed TikTok on other social media platforms such as Instagram to drive traffic to the platform and create viral content.

TikTok has also made creating content easy and fun. This has allowed users who may not have any previous experience or skills in editing videos to push their content out and receive positive engagement. All users are required to do is record a simple task or random moment in their daily routine and post it immediately. Furthermore, because all videos are short-form, it does not take a lot of time to shoot a video, and neither does it take time to watch one. Within an hour, a user could have easily watched up to 240 different videos offering different forms of entertainment. The benefit of having video content on-demand is that there are always users glued to the platform—the latest research showed that an average user stays on TikTok for 52 minutes each day (Mohsin, 2020b).

Using "For You" Page to Your Benefit

Upon opening the TikTok app, you will find a tab with videos that app labels "For You." For You videos are a compilation of videos that have been selected for you and recommended by TikTok. These videos are chosen based on the videos the user has viewed and those that match their particular interests. The interesting part about these videos is that they are from accounts that the user does not follow. However, because these videos are suited to the user's personal taste, they are more likely to enjoy the videos and follow the accounts thereof.

Therefore, it becomes clear why so many TikTok users dream of having their videos featured on the For You page; it is a great accomplishment for the average user and an opportunity to grow an influencer's brand. For an influencer, a video feature on the For You page would mean that the platform recognizes the entertainment value and quality of their content. It would also become a great opportunity to gain brand recognition by reaching an audience that did not previously know about them. Ultimately, it is one of the milestones that individuals will cross when becoming an influencer on TikTok.

Many individuals try to find tricks and tips on how to be featured on the For You page. The good news is that there is no trick or hidden code that you need to unlock to become recognized by the platform. The simple and obvious solution is to increase the quality of your content. Similarly to Instagram's Explore page, TikTok's For You page will simply recommend content with high engagement from users within your region. In other words, TikTok will reward you for keeping your followers engaged with your videos for a long time. This also means that you need to improve the performance ranking of your TikTok videos.

The performance ranking is founded on the percentage of the video that viewers watch (video completion ratio) and the number of comments, likes, and shares that the video receives. Thus, it is crucial to ensure that these short-form videos are packed with quality from start to finish for viewers to stay glued to your video and increase its overall performance. Below is a list of tips to help you improve on the performance of your TikTok content:

1. **Focus on Creating High-Quality Content**

One of the most important requirements for your content appearing on TikTok's For You page is to make sure that it is of the highest quality and rich in entertainment value. Low-quality, grainy videos can't appear on the platform's largest selection of trending videos. Producing high-quality content has become easier for many individuals due to the access to quality smartphones. However, even when the footage is appealing, the quality of the video extends to its content. This means that the stories that you share in your 15-second videos should be relatable, humorous, and appeal to the wider TikTok community.

2. Produce Shorter Videos

Even though TikTok videos are already fairly short, shortening your video's length further will encourage viewers to watch the entire video until the end and thus improve the video completion ratio. Of course, shortening your videos' length does not mean that you should compromise on the quality of your video or the entertainment value. Your video will still need to be long enough to tell a quick story and share your message across to others in the best form possible.

3. Include Music in Your Videos

Music will always be a part of the TikTok experience just as much as it formed a significant part of the Musical.ly experience. I would even go as far as saying that TikTok is perhaps better suited for music sharing than other popular social networking sites. The platform offers its users a plethora of music selections from various genres, providing users with ample assistance in creating great content. Music is commonly added as a background soundtrack that accompanies the video content. When users cannot find the soundtrack they are looking for on TikTok, they can edit a piece of music from their own device onto their videos. I would also advise influencers to remain updated on the trending soundtracks that users utilize in their videos because this trend changes all the time. To gain more traction on your video content, make sure that you shoot a video using the trending soundtracks as they go viral.

4. Add Hashtags

Adding hashtags to your videos will enhance engagement because they are more likely to be seen when users search for videos under popular or niche-specific hashtags. Some of the best hashtags to help your video receive views is by tagging the For You page in any one of these formats: #foryou, #fyp, #foryoupage.

5. Create Engaging Content

Regardless of your videos' quality, your content should always focus on matters or interests that your audience can relate to. Because TikTok customizes each user's For You page to appeal to their unique interests, you do not have to fear that your brand's message or story will be irrelevant or inappropriate for the TikTok community. Hence, it is always a great idea to focus on your brand's niche and produce quality content focusing on finding entertainment value within your particular industry. Your custom videos will appeal to a smaller audience within the larger TikTok community; however, you will receive a higher amount of engagement on your videos, helping you to create viral content.

Setting Up Influencer Marketing on TikTok

TikTok is undeniably growing at an accelerated rate, and because of this rapid growth, there are many opportunities presented for influencer marketing on the platform. Marketing opportunities are still new, and brands—along with influencers—are trying to learn as much as they can on how to use the platform to promote their message. Nevertheless, there are already many promotional advertising formats available for increasing exposure and promoting branded products or services.

1. **In-feed Ads**

In-feed video adverts merge within user feeds, and they operate on three models that include, cost-per-click (CPC), cost-per-impression (CPM), as well as cost-per-view (counted after six seconds of the video has been watched). Brands also have the luxury of creating a target profile, which the advert seeks to reach based on the audience's age, gender, or geographical location. To run in-feed adverts, brands can expect to pay $10 cost-per-impression with an imposed minimum campaign spend of $6,000.

2. **Brand Takeover Ads**

As the name suggests, brand takeovers are opportunities for brands to take charge of an entire category on TikTok for the day. As a rule, however, TikTok will only allow brands to take over one category (this could be food, fitness, fashion, or beauty) Users will be confronted with brand takeover ads as soon as they open their TikTok app, which helps brands receive the kind of reaction and attention that they desire. The main objective of brand takeover ads is to encourage users to click-through on the call-to-action included with the video, which would lead them to a third party website or landing page (sometimes it can lead them to the brand's profile within TikTok). Users have the option not to take any action. In this case, they would simply choose to skip the ad and continue on the next page, which would be the For You page. The cost of brand takeovers is $50,000 per day, with a guaranteed ROI of 5 million video impressions.

3. TikTok Hashtag Challenge Ads

These kinds of adverts take TikTok challenges and place them in an advertising format. The main purpose of hashtag challenge adverts is to encourage user-generated content by promoting a branded hashtag with instructions on how to complete and submit the brand's challenge. This type of advert would first appear as a banner on the For You page, and upon clicking on it, the user would proceed to a page with detailed instructions on how to participate in the brand's challenge. The benefit of using this kind of advert is that it guarantees a greater amount of impressions on videos with the branded hashtag, allowing for the brand's campaign to receive the desired engagement.

4. Branded TikTok Stickers

Another unique way of promoting a brand on TikTok is to create stickers that would, in effect, encourage audience members to engage with the brand's video content. Branded stickers are usually found in a user's video creation tool within the effects folder. These stickers are then easily added on videos, offering a more interactive experience with the brand. I find that branded stickers work best during brand events or special festivals when users are more encouraged to produce seasonal or event-specific content. For instance, a musician who is going on tour can create a branded sticker that fans can use on their videos in support or recognition of the musician's tour.

5. Influencer Marketing Ads

Influencer marketing adverts are among the most effective ways for brands to work with TikTok influencers to create their desired buzz or gain brand recognition. The TikTok influencer would leverage their following to help brands connect with their target audience in an entertaining and light-hearted way. Successful influencer marketing ads are those where the influencer has the creative freedom to design the most engaging content for the advert. Great partnerships are also fostered when the brand shares similar interests to the influencer, creating an authentic collaboration (and seen in how natural the influencer is in promoting the brand).

Many brands have already seen how effective influencer marketing can be on TikTok. Similarly, more influencers see how lucrative it can be to promote branded content on their TikTok profiles. With the partnership between brands and influencers growing stronger with every successful campaign, both brands and influencers study effective influencer marketing strategy. Below are just three steps that I have detailed, which can help both parties create an impactful branded campaign on TikTok.

Step 1: Understand How TikTok Works

To have a successful influencer marketing strategy on TikTok, you would first need to assess whether TikTok is the most appropriate social media platform for your brand.

This would involve researching the target audience that frequently uses TikTok and finding out their purpose for being on this platform. Moreover, you would need to explore the many ways of reaching your target audience on TikTok using the various TikTok trends or their advertising formats.

Step 2: Have Clear Campaign Goals

It is important to consider what you hope to achieve with your TikTok campaign before you begin marketing yourself. There are many goals that brands can strive for. For instance, they can either seek to drive user-generated content or encourage users to download their app, purchase products from their store, or visit their websites. Furthermore, brands need to establish clear and measurable key performance indicators (KPI), which will allow brands to measure the success of their TikTok campaign.

Step 3: Measure the Campaign Results

A campaign's success can only be determined by how well it performs. Therefore, I recommend brands and influencers to research the general benchmark of a high performing video and measure the success of their videos with this benchmark in mind. It would also be useful to research how competitors are sharing content (how long their videos are, what message they are sharing, and what trends they are using). Knowing how your competitors are engaging with other TikTokers will help you to test and optimize your content.

Strategies to Increase Follower Count

We all know that nowadays, there are so many opportunities to build a successful brand online. Popular social media platforms have opened a lucrative channel for influencers to establish their brands and help to spread awareness about brands and the products and services they offer. The opportunity for influencers to grow on platforms such as TikTok is expanding every day as more and more users download the app and seek to connect with like-minded people. TikTok allows for influencers to become overnight superstars gaining millions of followers with a single viral video. However, with the ever-increasing popularity of the app, gaining followers has become competitive. This is because there is a lot more content shared across the platform, and therefore gaining the necessary recognition is becoming a challenge. The strategies below will help you cut through the noise and allow your video content to be seen, thereby improving your chances of gaining more followers organically.

Strategy 1: Select a Specific Niche

Have you ever heard the saying, "Jack of all trades, master of none?" It refers to an individual who has split their focus and tinkered with many skills instead of focusing their mind on one skill and becoming an expert. I find that on TikTok, users who post random video content tend to get lost in the noise and seldom make a name for themselves. Only those who find a specific niche on the platform become known for their distinct content. It can be tempting to copy the kind of content that most users are posting and believe that this will help you gain recognition. Following the crowd seems advantageous at first, but soon you will realize that to influence the crowd, you cannot walk in the same direction as it. Ask yourself what your interests are and the most authentic way to show your funny or silly side on video. Stick to your niche and represent your brand to the best of your ability.

Strategy 2: An Attractive Profile Gains Followers

It is a common theme with all social media platforms that an appealing profile gains attention. There are many ways that you can optimize your TikTok profile to help you convert visitors into followers. For instance, create a cool username, pick the best profile picture, and ensure that your bio and any other information shared on your profile emphasize your brand's identity and message well. In essence, your profile page display must communicate the value that you can potentially offer followers. This value is seen in your layout, video content, quality of your footage, music selection, color schemes, and visual effects on videos. Therefore, you must consider the smaller details and pay attention to what your page is communicating about you.

Strategy 3: Post Consistently

TikTok is not short of content; there is so much video content uploaded every hour that it makes it difficult for a piece of content to stand out. Therefore, I recommend that influencers post regularly on TikTok, focusing on the quantity of content released as much as they focus on the quality. Indeed, it is not too much of a hassle to shoot a 15-second video every day, although influencers who strive to make the TikTok algorithm work in their favor will push to release three to 10 pieces of content every day. Nonetheless, I believe that it is better to post consistently instead of posting large quantities of content sporadically. Take time to decide on how many videos you can commit to posting consistently. Perhaps in the beginning, it can be twice a day, and as your page grows, you can increase the amount of content you post each day.

Strategy 4: Post Content During Peak Hours

Even though there is content shared on the platform throughout the day, there is still a peak hour where many users are active online and engaging with others within the community. Influencers should seek to post their content during these peak hours to increase their video's engagement rate. There are two peak hours on TikTok, and these are 11 a.m. and around 5:30 p.m. Another important consideration that you need to make when choosing posting times is to consider your target audience's behaviors, assessing how frequently they use TikTok and at what times. Doing this research will help you maximize the amount of exposure your content receives and allow it to reach the right people at the right time.

Strategy 5: Share Your TikTok Videos on Other Social Media Platforms

This strategy is highly effective in driving traffic to your TikTok profile and video content. Sharing your TikTok videos on other social media platforms allows you to target audiences who may not be on TikTok. It is also a great way to show your Facebook or Instagram followers the many different ways that you can create meaningful content. Users from other platforms will be interested in visiting your TikTok page because they are typically unfamiliar with TikTok's short-form video-sharing model. This will ultimately give you a great opportunity to convert followers or visitors from other social media channels into TikTok followers by giving them a sample of what they can expect by following your TikTok page.

Strategy 6: Use Popular Music

Music has a way of allowing strangers to connect through sharing a common taste in musical genres. I have often found that the best icebreaker in an unfamiliar setting is to have conversations about musical tastes or new music releases that have come out. As an influencer, you can build relationships with your audience by connecting through shared tastes in music. Of course, it would be counter-intuitive to select music that you do not enjoy listening to and using it as your background soundtrack. This would make you attract audiences that are not part of your brand's scope. Therefore, you should instead find popular soundtracks from the music genres that you love and use these popular tunes to create an entertaining video.

Strategy 7: Do not Be Afraid to Stand Out

The one drawback about TikTok that is seen as an opportunity for an influencer is that there is a lot of copied content. Copying is so prevalent on feeds that it has become an acceptable practice and a way to make a rendition or replicate a popular video. Everyone wants to emulate a viral video, and so you should aim to create viral content. To do this, you will need to post original content that has been well-considered and provides an entertainment value that will make your video shareable. My advice to you then would be to be yourself and allow your personal brand to shine. Share content that speaks to your brand's values and influence how other TikTok users create their content.

Creating a TikTok Trend

TikTok is by far the most exciting platform to be a part of on the Internet. Many young people, brands, and influencers are racking their brains, wondering how to leverage this unique video-sharing platform. Furthermore, we are witnessing more and more brands ditch the traditional forms of advertising and embracing newer digital spaces hoping to retain their customers or followers online. One of the best steps to take as a brand or influencer in establishing your marketing efforts on social media platforms such as TikTok is to understand the kind of content that the community enjoys and loves to engage with. You don't need to be a marketer to know that a video on current political or social affairs would not perform as well as a video of a dance challenge or a dog in a costume would on TikTok.

Therefore, connecting with the TikTok community requires brands and influencers to understand the kind of content that audiences resonate with and commit to posting as much of this content as possible. What marketers have also found to be true on TikTok, is that beautiful content is not necessarily enough to encourage viewership. Instead, the content has to be both beautiful and relatable. The generation of young people who are the main audience demographic on TikTok is more interested in finding content that will make them laugh or feel understood. It is more about personally envisioning themselves in the creator's shoes that allow this audience to connect with the content.

One of the most powerful ways of creating relatable content on TikTok is to create a trend or jump on an existing trend. Trending content inspires collective participation. It will mobilize users to replicate the trend and create their unique interpretations of it. The kind of content that can easily trend are videos of content creators lip-syncing, dancing, performing comedy skits, or pranks. This kind of content is entertaining, but it is also easily copied and thus promotes user-generated content. There are many trends that influencers can consider initiating, which will inspire other users to share their video, making it go viral and become the next most emulated content. Below are a few trends that you can consider for your next TikTok video:

1. **Create a Branded Hashtag Challenge**

TikTok relies heavily on hashtags to filter through different types of content. However, hashtags can easily become an interactive game on the platform too. Hashtag challenges use curated hashtags by brands or influencers, to motivate individuals in creating a themed video related to the particular campaign or viral trend. An amazing brand case study is Chipotle, who used the branded hashtag challenge to promote their hashtag #GuacDance. Users who were fans of the brand or who loved avocados used the hashtag #GuacDance to create a dance to the song "Guacamole Song" by famous children's entertainer Dr. Jean. This challenge resulted in 250,000 submissions, and this viral trend also led to an increase in guacamole sales as a side dish on orders at Chipotle.

Influencers can learn several lessons from the success of the #Guacdance. Firstly, it is important to keep the challenge easy to follow. Ensure that the instructions to complete the challenge are straightforward and easily replicable. For instance, if you decide to do a dance challenge, ensure that the dance moves that you desire for users to replicate are not too intricate or advanced for users to follow. Secondly, the challenge should always look fun. Nobody will want to replicate a challenge that seems boring or has been done in the past. Keep your challenge fun by finding new and original ways to help audiences interact with products or services. Lastly, a successful challenge will have a meaningful goal in mind. This would require you to establish whether the challenge will seek to bring brand awareness or promote existing or new products and launches.

2. Create an Educational Video

Contrary to popular beliefs, TikTok is not merely a platform where young people go to be goofy. The TikTok community is so large that there is a variety of interests and video content that users will find depending on their personal interests. This means that there is a market on the platform for sharing informative and educational content communicated in an easy-to-follow manner. Social activists, charities, brands in the health, finance, or technological industries can benefit from sharing relevant information on topics that affect young people.

3. Celebrate Special Events

Capitalizing on special occasions on the calendar can be a great way to make trending content. Usually, when it is a public holiday or special event, TikTok will create a custom hashtag to celebrate that holiday or event. For instance, TikTok has, in the past, celebrated International Women's Day, which is on the 8th of March with the hashtag #SheCanDoIt, which recognized the talent and work of female creators. This custom hashtag encouraged many users to post themed content in support of women's rights and honor all of the valiant women in history. As an influencer, you can use these custom hashtags to share your brand message at important times of the year or in people's lives.

4. Create a Tutorial

Tutorials can be a great form of content that helps users learn how to perform a skill. One of the most popular types of tutorials we have witnessed online is makeup tutorials, which seeks to teach audiences the tricks and tips on applying makeup. However, beauty is not the only type of skill that an influencer can teach through a tutorial. For instance, you can teach your followers how to pronounce certain words and phrases in your language, how to cook a particular recipe or share great workout tips for achieving specific fitness goals. In essence, any activity or skill that you learn by watching a short video clip can become a tutorial.

5. Do a Duet

Many of the TikTok users were previous Musical.ly subscribers, and thus there is a natural affinity for singing and performing song renditions. A popular type of content that frequently trends is watching two TikTokers perform a duet. The feature to perform duets without having to be in one location at the same time developed in 2018 by the platform. This feature allows users to create videos of them singing a part of a song and play them in a split-screen video format alongside another singing video of their choosing. Sometimes the duets can be with friends, celebrities, or other times with random users who are still part of the TikTok community.

Chapter 8: How to Pitch to Companies

We know that one of the reasons that have led to the growth of influencer marketing in recent years is the lack of trust that consumers show toward branded content released by companies. In fact, in 2018, as much as 25.2% of United States Internet users had blocked advertisements from their technological devices. Instead, social media influencers started becoming the trusted source for learning new skills, finding inspiration, or receiving great recommendations for products or services. Each influencer offers a unique value proposition, and their personal brands help distinguish their distinct message, style, and goals.

Consumers choose to follow influencers based on a shared belief system, style, or interests. It is easier for influencers to promote branded products because it is promoted by someone whom the customer believes in and relates to. Therefore, brands have increased their spending on influencer marketing due to the undeniable power these influencers have in directing customers to purchase products or to support brands. Most brands still view social media as a low-cost marketing tool, and therefore, it is rare to find brands whose entire marketing budget goes toward investing in an influencer. Typically, brands will contract influencers to help increase sales or the visibility of their brand online through strategic product placement.

Brands generally choose influencers based on their audience's size, their rate of engagement, and will then proceed to negotiate a partnership for a specific campaign. During the campaign, the company's marketing team will track and measure the influencer's performance and the extent to which the campaign meets the desired objectives and metrics. When influencers do not meet the desired campaign goals, they are simply not assigned another campaign with that particular brand. In this case, the brand would look for another influencer for its next campaign. It is common to find brands liaising directly with influencers; however, sometimes, brands communicate with influencers through third-party agencies that manage them.

Transactional versus Relationship-based Influencer Marketing

Influencers need to know the difference between a transactional and a relationship-based influencer marketing strategy because brands are most likely to contract an influencer under one of these umbrellas. A transactional influencer marketing strategy focuses on acquiring an influencer for a certain online campaign without any obligation to contact them again. Brands who opt for a transactional approach do not necessarily look for a brand ambassador but more so a face or an influential voice to appear on a specific campaign. Usually, the two parties will negotiate the expectations and come up with a great marketing plan. Once the campaign is over, the influencer is also free to represent other brands. This type of influencer marketing strategy does not require brands to build trust with their influencers because contracts are short, and terms and conditions are enforced.

The second kind of approach is the relationship-based influencer marketing strategy. In this approach, the brand is more concerned about selecting an influencer whose target audience is aligned to the brand's audience and in making sure that the influencer's reach is large enough to connect with potential customers. This type of strategy contracts influencers for an extended time, which helps both parties build a strong relationship with each other and help the influencer's audience build a meaningful connection with the brand. Most influencers will lean toward these kinds of agreements with brands (if they are presented with a choice) because they provide greater job security due to the extended time frames. Brands are also willing to give influencers creative freedom in designing a successful campaign (which meets all of the brand's KPI's).

The Influencer - Brand Relationship

Landing a brand partnership is an exciting time in an influencer's career because it marks the beginning of monetizing their personal brands. Micro-influencers do not need to feel intimidated by larger influencers. Nowadays we see a lot of brands favoring the small fish and using them in their campaigns. However, developing such partnerships requires more than just growing your follower count on social media platforms. We need to remember that brands are businesses, and every marketing effort must be accounted for and help them convert potential customers into purchasing customers. This means that as lovely as an influencer's brand is, brands need to look at many other factors before deciding if the influencer is the most appropriate brand to leverage to bring a strong ROI.

1. You Need to Look the Part

As an influencer, your brand needs to look the part to attract potential clients. When I say "look the part," I am essentially referring to your brand's image and how it reflects online. Brands will swarm toward influencers whose personal brands are aspirational or display a desirable lifestyle. For instance, if you are a fashion influencer, you need to put together the most stylish looks and be creative in the locations that you choose to shoot your photos. Ultimately, when a brand chooses to use you as the face of their campaign, they trust you to increase the desirability of their product or service rather than diminish it with a poorly managed personal brand.

Looking the part does not require you to become superficial or design content that you are not comfortable with. Instead, it requires you to be consistent in the quality of content and the style that your brand represents. Another benefit of being consistent early on is that you can have an in-depth story to share with brands about who you are and the value you can offer. For instance, a fashion influencer who does not post any photos of them wearing stylish clothes will not be able to successfully convince brands they are capable of marketing the brand's clothing. Influencers should prioritize polishing their personal brands and pushing out quality content for free before they can expect to approach brands for partnerships.

Maintaining your personal brands while building your credibility will be a costly job. This is because you might need to invest in paid advertising, a camera, video editing software subscriptions, purchasing props, clothes, food, makeup, or any other accessory that will help you create great content. Having to pay to maintain your brand can become a stressful task if you do not have a source of income. Therefore, I recommend you keep your day job if you have one because you will need to invest your own capital at the beginning of your influencer journey.

2. Know Your Value

The most common advice I hear in response to the question of how to approach brands is that the influencer should know their value. This kind of advice is broad and hardly gives the influencer any direction to take. Therefore, to understand what it means to know your value, we can see value as the ultimate display of usefulness. So in rephrasing the commonly expressed advice, we can now say that when influencers approach brands, they need to know how they can be useful. Before contacting a brand with a beautifully written pitch, you need to ask yourself this sobering question—what makes me valuable to this brand? You should be able to answer this question within seconds, leaving no room for hesitation.

Realizing how your brand is useful not only to brands but to your community of followers, requires a lot of time building your brand and sharing your content with others. This is because your worth is not established before you can begin your journey. Instead, it is discovered through constant engagement with your community and noticing the big and small ways your brand makes a difference in others' lives. Therefore, when your personal brand is still in its infancy stage, it is impossible to know what value you bring to the table. Knowing your value will take experience, and yes, experience requires time. How much time do you ask? Enough time to drive meaningful traffic to your social media accounts and build a reputation for being or doing something useful.

3. Build Relationships with Brands Before You Need Them

It is always good to build relationships with brands before you send them a cold email requesting for work. The truth is that no one will see you doing it because it will be behind the scenes, but forming these relationships will be evident for everyone to see. It goes back to the simple truth that people do business with people that they like. Your likeability as an influencer must have been a result of previous positive interactions with the brand. You can start building relationships with brands that you one day hope to work with by following their social media accounts, tagging them in content where you are interacting with their brand, or directly engaging with their online community. Soon these brands will notice your page and see a lot of similarities in what you offer and what they need. The best-case scenario is that the brand begins to engage with you online and thus begin to form a relationship.

Pitching to Brands

Influencers are more likely to receive attention from brands when they go out of their way to pitch to them—unless you are Kylie Jenner and brands come flocking to you. You would be surprised to know that even with the growth of influencer marketing and the popularity of using influencers for branded content, only a few influencers receive a continuous flow of inbound work. The best way to create a portfolio of work for yourself is to approach brands with ideas and suggestions of collaborations. Directly pitching to brands or through the agencies that represent brands, influencers have an opportunity to finally reveal their crafted personal brands to the marketers who would benefit the most from leveraging it.

Therefore, an influencer should plan for this moment and prepare themselves to contact the brands that they desire to work for. To successfully pitch your personal brand to these potential clients, you need to understand the fundamental principles of a great pitch. Great pitches are strategic in that they will include all of the information needed to convince the brand to follow-up and request more information. You will not receive an immediate "Yes!" from the initial pitch, however, when successful, you will receive an opportunity to sit down with the brand for a formal interview or discussion—this should be your only expectation from the pitch. Below are useful steps that you can take to prepare a powerful pitch:

Step 1: Do Your Homework on the Brand

The first step requires that you research the brand that you desire to work with. During this research phase, you would need to assess whether the brand's identity aligns with your personal brand and whether both of you share similar interests and values.

Another important factor to look into is whether you and the desired brand have the same target audience. I recommend that you only pitch to brands that share an almost identical representation of your target audience because. It will significantly increase the likelihood of the brand responding to your pitch.

Moreover, you need to analyze the brand's social media accounts to find more valuable information to guide you on your pitch. Firstly, you should notice which social media platforms the brand is on and ensure that your brand is also on the majority of them. Once you are on their social media profiles, look for any prior marketing campaigns that used influencers. If the brand's previous marketing campaigns have no evidence of using influencer marketing, you would need to state this observation in your pitch so that you do not look ill-informed. Their social media pages will also show you the products or services that the brand is currently promoting and contact information that will link you to the best department to speak to PR, sales, marketing, or community manager.

Step 2: Be Specific

Generic pitches will not receive any kind of response from brands. This is because a generic pitch can look like spam or an unprofessional and dispassionate document. The truth is that brands want to work with influencers who are enthusiastic about the brand and desire to bring value. Your pitch cannot merely state that you desire to collaborate; instead, it should specify the many suggestions you have of successful collaborations. I also find that detailed pitches are easier to draft when the influencer has a clear understanding of the potential client's goals. Go onto their social media pages or read recent blog posts and articles to assess the direction of the brand and what their marketing needs are at this moment in time.

Each brand is different; therefore, each pitch will offer brands a different value proposition. Once again, your value proposition would be based on the needs of the brand you already identified. I would also encourage you to be specific on the strengths that you bring to the table. Perhaps you are an influencer who can take professional photography, and thus you would be able to shoot and edit your own content. Adding your strengths and any skill that can minimize the expense of hiring you as an influencer will play in your favor and help you deliver a pitch that is very difficult to refuse.

Step 3: Position Yourself as an Industry Expert

Showing brands that you understand the industry that they are participating in will strengthen your pitch. It will make you come across as someone who has gained a considerable amount of experience as an influencer which is great for brands. They will not need to spend time training you on how digital marketing works, or they can use you as a trusted guide in helping them understand how digital marketing works. The more information you know about the brand, its industry, and how influencer marketing can boost its sales, the more valuable you become to the brand (it can also open other opportunities to collaborate with the brand in the future).

How you can position yourself as an industry expert is to explain to brands why influencer marketing would be the best approach for their brand right now and all of the opportunities it can present in engaging with their target audience. You can then share reasons why you would be the perfect influencer to lead one of their campaigns and help them meet their marketing objectives. Adding statistics and recent customer data can help to convince brands on the importance of influencer marketing. Ultimately, your goal in positioning yourself as an expert is to show brands that your personal brand is professional and you are trustworthy enough to deliver on the set metrics and objectives of a particular campaign.

Influencer Pitch Templates

There is no standard format to use when pitching to brands; most of the time, influencers design their pitches by finding creative ways to share their personality with the brand while also sharing relevant information. I believe that the main outcome that all influencers should aim for is to break the ice and create an initial connection with the brand. As I mentioned before, you should not expect brands to respond with a contract attached to their email asking you to sign on the dotted line. A pitch is usually the first point of contact (or second if you have been engaging with the brand online), and thus you should expect many more face-to-face or virtual discussions before a brand decides to take you on as their influencer. Nonetheless, below are some amazing pitch templates that will help you begin thinking about how you would like to present your pitch to your desired brand. You are welcome to use these templates as they are presented; however, your pitch would appear more special if you personalize the template by adding your own personality.

1. Template for Pitching to a Brand as a New Influencer

Hey [Brand name]!

I have been a supporter of [Brand name] for almost three years now and [State why you are loyal to the brand]. In particular, I truly love how [Mention a specific quality or value about the brand that you genuinely enjoy].

My [insert the social media platform you would like to use to represent the brand] audience consists of 85% [Insert similarities in demographics] who would love your products.

Furthermore, my [Insert another social media platform that you would like to use to represent the brand] receives an average engagement of [Add social media analytics]. Therefore, I believe that with a clear marketing plan, we could achieve [State some objectives or goals that you can help the brand achieve].

I would appreciate the opportunity to continue this conversation about how I can promote your amazing products on my social media accounts.

I look forward to your favorable response.

[Your email signature]

2. Template for Pitching to a Brand for a Free Travel Stay

Hi [Company name],

Thank you for taking the time to open my email. My name is [Your name], and I am a travel blogger running the popular travel blog [Link to your blog or website]. I am currently organizing a vacation to [Location] on [Date]. I would like my vacation to be an opportunity to partner with a local hotel during my visit, and I thought yours would be ideal.

I came across your hotel [Background information], and I knew from that moment that my blog community would love to experience what it is like to stay at your hotel. I particularly believe that the readers would love [Enter specific highlights or features of the hotel that would appeal to your target audience].

Currently, my blog generates [Blog statistics] of traffic per month, and my Pinterest and Instagram has over [Social media statistics] of followers and an engagement rate of [Social media statistics].

In return for a complimentary stay while I am on vacation, I would be more than happy to offer you a hotel review article on my blog, three Instagram photographs with rich descriptions on my feed, and [add all of the content that you would offer for free as part of the deal]. I would also offer you free access to use the content that I generate at your hotel as part of your own marketing material, whether it is for a campaign, marketing resources such as pamphlets, or as part of your public relations content.

I look forward to hearing from you!

[Your email signature]

3. Template for Pitching to a Brand for Product Collaboration

Greetings [Brand name]!

I have used [Product name] religiously in the last couple of years [State why you have used their product—list the product benefits].

You may have noticed how much I regularly post about your brand on my various social media channels [Insert link to your social media accounts], and the questions that I have received from my community about [Name the specific product].

I have a history of working with brands such as X, Y, and Z. Due to my 100,000 followers on [Name the various social media channels] and my [Add social media analytics such as engagement rate and number of views per post], I was able to help brand X increase their sales by 68% and brand Y [List some factual data from your previous campaigns].

It would be such an amazing collaboration to work with you in promoting [Name the specific product] to my enthusiastic followers on [Name the various social media channels]. I would love for us to meet virtually or face-to-face to share with you some of my collaboration ideas.

Thank you for your time!

[Your email signature]

Common Mistakes to Avoid When Pitching to Brands

Knowing how to pitch to brands is vital in forming a favorable first impression with the brand. A successful pitch will allow you to present your personal brand in the best light possible. From your clear and detailed pitch, brands would have received the necessary information to assess whether you can offer the kind of value they are looking for. Think of your pitch as the make-or-break moment that will decide whether you continue discussions about representing the brand or moving along to the next one. The importance of a great pitch should not intimidate you because most of the information you will be sharing is related to your brand's value offer. Your information will also include the statistics you have gathered from your social media accounts and other sites such as your blog or website. Below are some common mistakes that you can note and avoid when designing your pitch to brands:

- ☐ **Don't make the pitch all about you.** Focus instead on how you can help the brand connect with your target audience.

- ☐ **Don't reach out to brands that you do not use or love.** Instead, focus on brands that you have already featured on your content or made reference to in some way.
- ☐ **Don't send your media kit straight away.** Brands should follow up with you by requesting your influencer media kit as this would show some level of willingness to work with you from their part.
- ☐ **Don't pitch through social media Direct Messages.** Social media should only be used to start a conversation or request more contact information (the email of the community manager).
- ☐ **Don't pitch to the wrong person.** Make sure that you have received the contact information of the individual who would handle influencer engagements.
- ☐ **Don't pitch if you are not prepared.** This includes pitching when your social media accounts have not gained any significant traffic, engagement, or influence.
- ☐ **Don't think that the brand knows who you are.** Take time to introduce yourself to the brand and present all of the necessary statistics that give your personal brand credibility.
- ☐ **Don't forget to clearly state the unique value that you can add to the brand.** Let brands know the details of the type of content you will post and the skills and talents that you bring to the table.
- ☐ **Don't provide too many frivolous details.** Remember that brand managers receive many emails each day, so you must focus on making yours stand out by only including useful information.
- ☐ **Don't forget to follow up with the brand.** Sometimes, managers can miss your email or forget to respond; therefore, if they have not gotten back to you within two weeks, you can follow up with them. If the brand manager does not respond to the follow-up email, you can take it as a sign that your pitch was unsuccessful. On to the next brand!
- ☐ **Don't forget to end the email on a strong note.** Remember to add a powerful call-to-action at the end of your email to encourage the brand manager to respond.

Chapter 9: How to Monetize Your Social Media Accounts

Social media is no longer a platform for merely sharing your quirky selfies or memes. Over the years, it has proven to brands to be an appropriate marketing channel for reaching out to their customers and spreading the word about their businesses. Social media has played such a significant role in brand outreach that it is unthinkable for a brand not to have any kind of social media presence. Any business can use various forms of social media as an effective marketing tool in growing their community of support online. However, when it comes down to it, all brands expect to see some sort of result in their marketing efforts.

In other words, every sponsored advert or branded content must, in some way, encourage visitors to convert to customers or lead individuals to the brand's website or app. In this context, the role of the influencer is to help the brand achieve this overarching goal of customer conversion and effectively increase their sales, brand awareness or brand reputation. Hence, brands are willing to pay influencers for the target audience exposure they give brands access to. An influencer's work is becoming more of a necessity than a luxury as social networking sites update their algorithms in support of quality engagement and user-generated content. Therefore, social media has become a win-win opportunity for brands to grow their businesses and influencers to generate a stable income.

I am sure you have heard of successful YouTubers or Instagram influencers who have earned millions through advertising branded products and services on their social media accounts. Some of these influencers were solo entrepreneurs who decided to sell their own products and services to their large community of followers. However, these thriving influencers are so few and far between. Majority of those who call themselves influencers today have not reached the levels of engagement or influence that these popular personal brands have. This isn't because they are not talented or that their content isn't good enough; instead, it is due to underestimating the importance of finding a niche and a specific target audience whose pain points your brand can solve.

It is easy for new influencers to become seduced by worrying about the number of followers they have. Focusing soley on your follower count will tempt you to post random content that seeks to advertise to many audiences and solve many needs. Making money on your social media accounts will require a more focused strategy favoring a community-centric approach. Your personal brand will not be everything to everyone, and this is okay. Having community members who share similar interests to you will strongly increase your levels of engagement because your content becomes valuable.

One of the rules you can remember when seeking to monetize your social media accounts is the 60/30/10 rule. This rule states that 60% of the content you post should always be valuable and interesting to your target audience and not be sales-oriented. This should include content that sparks a conversation, inspires, or educates your followers. Moreover, 60% of your content should be shareable, and therefore it must be of high-quality and unique enough to get people talking. A further 30% of your content should be content that is shared from other sources, such as brands or businesses that are not your competition.

This could also include content shared from your online community (such as user-generated content). If you see any content online that may be relevant to your target audience, you should consider sharing it. There is also the possibility of members returning the favor by sharing your original content. Either way, sharing other useful content will make your brand relatable, dynamic, and focused on serving your audience's needs. Lastly, 10% of your social media content should be sales-oriented. You may think that sharing only 10% of promotional content is little; however, when your social media accounts sound like a huge sales pitch, you are less likely to make any sale. When your community receives genuine value, only then will they be enthusiastic about purchasing any promotional product or service.

Monetizing Your YouTube Page

So you have now mastered working YouTube's algorithm, your video SEO is top-notch, and you have a decent amount of traffic coming onto your page. At this point, you have reached a milestone that most influencers long to obtain—you are now ready to monetize your YouTube account! However, before you can begin making money from your video content, you need to understand the monetization policies that are put in place on the platform. The first step is to qualify for monetization. Your page qualifies to generate income when you have at least 4,000 hours of video content watched within the last year and at least 1,000 YouTube subscribers on your page.

In other words, YouTube prioritizes engagement above the number of traffic that your page receives. It is also a way to ensure that content creators work hard to produce as much content as they can before earning money from it—the more work you put in to build your brand and create high-quality content, the greater your chances of making money in the future. Now that you know the criteria to apply for monetization, you should begin optimizing your page immediately. However, in the interim, there are other available options for making money using your influence on YouTube.

1. Patronage

Patreon is among the popular online patronage platforms, allowing loyal fans to pay a monthly subscription to view exclusive content from their favorite YouTubers. Of course, you can imagine how spectacular your content should be for any fan to pay to see more of it every month. Patreon even allows you to create tiers of patrons, and in each tier, you can provide a variety of never-before-seen footage that regular non-paying followers would not be able to see. You can be as creative as you want with the exclusive content you provide your loyal paying fans, ensuring that you keep them wanting to access more content every month.

2. Merchandise

People love to own branded merchandise, especially when it is from an influencer that they adore. Selling merchandise, such as branded t-shirts or caps is a great way for you to make money from your growing list of followers on YouTube. Although, I advise that you start small and test the response of your community before you order thousands of merchandise with no sizable demand. For instance, you can ask your audience whether they would be interested in purchasing a cool t-shirt or even go as far as asking them to suggest the type of merchandise that they would buy and wear. In other words, the process from designing to selling should be interactive with your audience to ensure that your stock is sold out within days (thereby prompting you to order more and continue generating an income).

3. Affiliate Marketing

Another way that you can make money from your YouTube channel is to apply for an affiliate program. Affiliate programs encourage you to promote another brand on your channel and drive traffic directly to the promoted brand's website. Usually, the brand will offer you a discount code that you can share with your followers, which will help you earn a commission every time your discount code is used. Even though influencers earn less money from affiliate marketing than they would from brand sponsorships, it is still a great place to start when you are new to the industry and seek to gain experience working with other brands.

4. Product Features

Many influencers will begin their career promoting branded products before they can sign contracts for brand sponsorships. An important cautionary note about product features is that sometimes brands will not pay you in cash to promote their products. Instead, they may choose to offer you coupons or free merchandise in exchange for a feature. As a new influencer, this should not be a deterrent; I mean, who doesn't love free products, right? You do not even need to wait for brands to approach you for product features because they are always looking to reach new customers online and increase their sales.

   5. **Paid Sponsorships**

I left paid sponsorships for last because it is perhaps the most lucrative way of making money on YouTube (even if you do not have a monetized YouTube channel yet). Paid sponsorships are when brands pay influencers to mention, discuss, or review their products or services in their videos. As much as paid sponsorships are a goldmine for generating an income on YouTube, we should not take them lightly because it can be difficult to convince a brand that you will deliver measurable results from a paid sponsorship. Influencers who have a proven track record of marketing for brands have a higher chance of being selected to represent more brands and get paid for doing it. Therefore, before you pitch to a company for a paid sponsorship, make sure that you have social proof that your brand is powerful at delivering brand objectives.

Monetizing Your Instagram Page

Instagram is arguably the largest image-sharing social media platform on the Internet today. Due to the emphasis on sharing photos, influencers need to put in a lot of work to produce content that can stand out from the sea of photography and videos. Making money through your Instagram page is not impossible; any individual who has put in the necessary consideration into their content can start making money before they reach tens of thousands of followers. Nonetheless, the standard of quality regarding photography is significantly high on Instagram with creatives using all sorts of equipment and editing software to produce mesmerizing content. An influencer seeking to monetize their Instagram page will, therefore, need to build a formidable brand that can attract an ideal community of followers.

Even though you don't need millions of followers to start earning money on Instagram, you are still required to have some level of influence. This means that micro-influencers are considered to be individuals with Instagram pages consisting of a minimum of 1,000 followers. The work does not stop after acquiring your first 1,000 followers. From here on out, you will need to convince Instagram's algorithm that your page has relevant and interesting content that your audiences would love to see. Secondly you need to show that you have a high engagement rate with your followers (sending them direct messages and commenting and liking their photos).

At this point, the multiplier of your success will be in sustaining a strong relationship with your followers and finding new ways of expressing your brand. Those who opted to buy followers when they set up their page will experience issues getting their followers to engage with them. This is because fake followers are not necessarily interested in your content or your brand as a whole. What ends up happening is that the influencer has a high number of inactive followers who do not like, comment, or share any of their content. Therefore, I strongly recommend that you instead sponsor your posts to attract your desired audience instead of buying followers and being caught up in a sticky predicament later on when engagement rate counts. Once you have solidified your brand and your customers consider you to be a friend rather than a foe, you can begin implementing some creative strategies of earning money.

1. Earn Money Through Photos

Earning money through your photography is one of the obvious ways of monetizing your Instagram page. For instance, if you have a decent follower count, and your engagement is good, your followers should be willing to follow the links when a clear call-to-action is inserted. Your photos become the bait that your followers latch onto and can then easily follow the instructions added to complete the desired action.

2. Earn Money as an Instagram Model

Influencers can also earn money by modeling merchandise from brands on their Instagram page. The benefit of being an Instagram model is that you do not have to look like the supermodels we see on famous runways. In essence, you will be required to show a brand's product or service in use. For instance, if you are a beauty influencer, you would need to wear the brand's makeup or give a tutorial on how to apply it. On the other hand, if you were an Instagram model for a brand selling camping gear, you would be expected to take photos while camping for the target audience to experience what it would be like sleeping in that brand's tent. Once again, being true to your personal brand will help you find the most suitable brand that you can authentically represent as their model.

3. Earn Money Reviewing Products

What makes influencers indispensable in brand campaigns is their power to influence their audience to act. When followers see their favorite influencer rocking a new pair of jeans and expressing their sentiments about the jeans, it makes followers want to own a pair as soon as possible. Perhaps this sales pitch would not have been as convincing if it came directly from the jean brand, but because it was validated by the influencer, the product became more desirable. Influencers can leverage this unique ability to drive consumers to make purchase decisions by offering reviews on branded products. These products should always remain within the niche that the influencer occupies, which will make the pitch come across as useful and provide valuable information for the audience to make a purchase decision.

4. Sell Your Own Products

Influencers can also leverage their personal brand to sell their merchandise instead of selling products for other brands. Many influencers have become successful entrepreneurs and brand ambassadors by finding their target audience and selling products directly to them. Not only do your followers get to form a personal relationship with your personal brand, but they will also get to experience your products. This makes the influencer's company become more personal and relatable. It allows the community to be excited about new product releases and willingly follow links to the online store or use promotional discount codes when they are presented with them. This strategy can also work in reverse; an entrepreneur can seek to create a strong personal brand online to form a solid relationship with their own brand's customers.

5. Earn Money Through Sponsored Posts

This is the most common way for influencers to make money on Instagram. Influencers may approach appropriate brands for sponsorship. On Instagram, sponsorship can take on many different forms because there are many types of media to use on the platform. The type of media used will be based on the brand's campaign strategy and how it seeks to communicate with its audience members. More and more brands are marketing through Instagram stories and inserting click-through links that viewers can follow. Other brands are sticking to the classical sponsored post that ensures the post receives high-quality engagement through likes, re-grams, and comments.

Monetizing Your Facebook Page

I find that Facebook is an attractive social media channel for influencers to use in making money, for the mere fact that it is the largest and most enduring social media platform. Facebook has rebranded itself many times in the past, each time improving the quality of the experience. I have found that the platform and its team of engineers are particularly interested in fulfilling its members' desires and ensuring that brands receive quality leads. However, to monetize your Facebook page as an influencer, there are a few guidelines that the platform has established that govern how you can monetize your page.

For instance, Facebook requires you to share authentic content that has been ideally created by yourself and which offers value to the community. Any kind of content that sounds fraudulent, hateful, inciting violence, or fear will be taken down by the platform and your page may be suspended. Facebook also has a number of guidelines indicating how a brand should interact with community members, guidelines on payment terms, and how your Facebook page can comply with the platform's rules. Once you have read through and agreed on the terms and conditions of monetizing your account, you can begin to explore the many ways of earning money on Facebook.

1. Drive Facebook Traffic to Your Blog

Influencers can earn money by directing their Facebook audience to their blogs by sharing snippets of blog articles and links to access it. To effectively do this, however, you need to ensure that your content is shareable and interesting. The greater the perceived value of your content, the better it tends to perform on Facebook feeds. You can also increase engagement on your content by making sure that you follow and engage with individuals who could be members of your target audience. For instance, Facebook will eventually track a pattern of visitors that your page receives, and it will create an audience for you. When this audience includes random individuals who are not a part of our target audience, our page analytics will be compromised. Therefore, I recommend that you become friends and join groups within your brand's particular niche (this could mean that you have to reject Aunt Jackie's friend request).

2. Earn Money From Facebook Groups

Compared to earning money using a Facebook page, monetizing a Facebook group may prove to be easier due to the greater amount of flexibility Facebook provides group admins in how they can frame the purpose of the group. For instance, you can label your group as a support group, thus making it appear as a valuable resource to your target audience. This would make your page seem like less of a sales or for-profit scheme and more of a community-centered space.

Audiences would be more willing to sign up and be a part of your group and see it as a safe place to engage in common group interests. Monetizing your Facebook group would require you to focus more on building your personal brand as an authority and valuable resource in sharing information or inspiring group members. Instead of immediately pushing promotional content, you would need to prioritize building brand advocates.

3. Facebook Video Monetization

In its efforts to continue improving the platform's quality, Facebook has developed a new way for brands and influencers to earn money from pushing video content. The benefit of using Facebook's video monetization platform is that the company pays you directly for quality video content that audiences desire to engage with and share. The more frequent and longer the viewers engage with your Facebook videos, the greater your videos will perform on facebook's algorithm, which rewards high engagement and meaningful relationships built between content creators and the community.

4. **Earn Money with Facebook Ads**

Influencers can also earn an income by promoting their own products or other brands through Facebook Ads. A Facebook advert aims to send a clear message prompting the ideal customer to act in a desired manner. Therefore, your adverts should be as informative and direct as possible. I would encourage you to continuously test your adverts' performance of your adverts and compare different campaigns alongside each other to find the best message, style, and call-to-action to use on your adverts. Furthermore, I would suggest that you don't spend your advertising budget on brand awareness campaigns, which are long-term investments that larger corporations or personal brands would benefit from. Instead, spend more of your budget creating your custom target audience, making it as specific to your ideal customer as possible.

Monetizing Your Pinterest Page

Pinterest has built a reputation over the years for being the go-to platform to find inspiration for new DIY projects, recipes, fashion styles, or products to purchase. Brands and influencers have capitalized on this platform by promoting desirable content that drives waves of visitors to their websites, e-commerce stores, apps, or blogs. However, successfully driving traffic to other third party websites will require your commitment to pinning inspirational and aesthetically pleasing content. Like many social media platforms, Pinterest has made updates to its algorithm to ensure that there is a standard to obtain when seeking to find and engage with followers.

For instance, Pinterest has changed how affiliate marketing and contests run to protect users from spam accounts or coming across illegal schemes, unverified websites, and other fraudulent online schemes. The change in algorithm has meant that those who had learned strategies to make money in the old system had to learn newer ways of posting and engaging with audiences. However, the new changes have brought about many opportunities for influencers to make money on the platform through a variety of ways listed below.

1. **Use Pinterest for Blogging**

Pinterest is a standard tool used by bloggers to direct organic and paid traffic to their blog site. Bloggers make money by increasing its subscribers, readership, page views and visitors engaging with sponsored advertising on the blog site. However, the money-making train begins with sharing a pin of your new blog article on Pinterest and making the photo and text appeal to your target audience's pain points. Another way to increase traffic to your blog is to create Pinterest boards that individually cater to different blog topics or categories (this may include tips, reviews, interviews, or general guidelines). You can also create collaborative boards where you pin a collection of niche-related articles from your favorite bloggers (and they would offer the same opportunity to you).

2. Collaborate with a Brand

Influencers can also work directly with brands to create collaborated pins. The brand would select an influencer whose Pinterest page has a similar audience and priorities as the brand. The content could be pinned on the brand's page to show the association with the influencer or pin it to the influencer's page to drive traffic to the brand's Pinterest page or other appropriate channels. I would also encourage influencers to approach brands with suggestions on Pinterest pins that would increase brand perception or provide the target audience with more information. For instance, you can pitch pin ideas like "10 ways to upcycle Coca-cola cans" or "5 recipes using Nestle cooking cream."

3. Gain a Skill and Monetize It

Your personal brand will need to constantly provide new creative ways of connecting with your target audience. Even though your personality will be enough to create a community, it will not be able to sustain your audience's needs and demands. Therefore, you should continue enriching yourself with the knowledge and skills to expand your brand's reach and, subsequently, your influence. Pinterest can help you earn more money by exposing you to new crafts, skills, or methods of perfecting your talent and gaining new ones too. Yes, this is an indirect way of earning money; however, it is a necessary investment that all influencers should make to secure their ability to earn a living in the future.

4. Drive Traffic to Your E-commerce Website

Due to the focus on photography, Pinterest has become a new hub for online retailers or those influencers who are representing online stores. In a way, online retailers are using Pinterest as a catalog to list and promote their merchandise. Fashion is a large category on the platform, and fashion bloggers are no strangers to highlighting new trends, styles, or tips on dressing up. Influencers now have the opportunity to model clothing or design beautiful fashion catalogs that can drive traffic to the online store. Instead of reading about various trends, users will be able to purchase trendy clothing through the influencer's pins. Another strategy to monetize your catalogs would be to partner with brands on affiliate programs. This way, you will earn money from every user who purchases merchandise advertised on Pinterest through your promotional code.

Monetizing Your TikTok Page

The rapid growth of TikTok over the years has made it an appealing marketing tool for businesses. To engage its young audience, brands have had to develop innovative content that can help them promote their brands while generating an income. TikTok influencers are not left behind in this bid to monetize the platform. We have seen content creators shift from merely consuming content to leveraging their TikTok popularity for brand sponsorships and promotions. An attractive TikTok influencer for a brand can produce high-quality and engaging content relevant to the brand's target audience. Below are some of the strategies that influencers can use to monetize their TikTok page.

1. **Brand Sponsorships**

For an influencer to bag a brand sponsorship, they will need to prove that their brand is influential. One of the best ways to prove this is by having an account with many followers that are all part of your particular niche or specialty. It may be quite difficult to convince a brand to work with you if you do not have a large follower count, and if your content does not have rich engagement. Therefore on TikTok, influencers need to continue working on growing their numbers and understanding the TikTok algorithm, which will help them improve on the performance and exposure of their content. Influencers with followers in the millions are highly attractive to brands; however, smaller businesses may also consider micro-influencers with a minimum follower count of 30,000.

2. **Directing Traffic to Other Sites**

Influencers can also make money by directing their TikTok audience to other websites and social media platforms. TikTok's primary audience is millennials, who are extremely active on most social media platforms. Influencers can work with brands to direct this energetic audience to other apps or platforms such as YouTube or Instagram, where they are met with more content or offers. Instead of using a lot of your advertising budget to find millennials on other platforms such as Facebook, you can market your content or insert links on TikTok where the majority of the community is young people.

3. **Shout Outs**

Research has shown us time and time again, how effective and powerful word of mouth advertising is. I believe that it is even more effective among millennials who rely heavily on peer reviews for making purchase decisions or supporting brands. Influencers with a large following can make money by giving other brands a shout out on their TikTok videos, in captions, or their bio. When a fan is recommended a product or service from their idol or role model, they are more likely to respond favorably out of sheer loyalty and trust formed with the influencer. Influencers can list their shout out services on platforms like Fiverr, where businesses go to find talent for their growing brands.

4. Create TikTok Videos Specifically for Businesses

TikTok influencers can find even more opportunities to generate revenue by promoting branded products and services in their short 15-second video clips. The best part about creating sponsored videos is that you do not need to be a mega influencer to hop on the bandwagon. For instance, you can approach smaller brands that would find micro-influencers more attractive (and affordable) than using larger influencers. I recommend that you offer to promote brands for free for a limited time only, to create an impressive portfolio of work experience and build trust with brands. Eventually, you will grow large enough to charge brands and they will be happy to pay you due to your proven track record of meeting marketing objectives.

Other great ways for influencers to make money from TikTok include downloading its sister app Live.ly, which allows users to live-stream directly to their TikTok followers. This live-streaming website allows viewers to make contributions to the influencer in the form of donations as a way to show appreciation for their content. Furthermore, TikTok now allows users to share links on their bios to direct audience members to other websites. We are still waiting for the platform to develop ways of monetizing the video content that users produce. With so many developments that have already taken place in the short amount of time that it has been around, I am certain that influencers will soon find more lucrative ways of earning an income through TikTok.

Chapter 10: Targeting Different Demographics with Different Social Media Platforms

Social media demographics are an important piece of information for influencers to know. This is mainly because these statistics show the type of audiences that use specific social media platforms. Understanding where your particular audience is among the various platforms will help you create targeted social media campaigns that are relevant to your audience's need on the specific social media network that they are on. For instance, you would rarely find a millennial looking for information on building a retirement fund; thus; those investment companies need to find an online audience of mature senior citizens and understand which social media platforms they spend most of their time and how they engage online.

The most unfortunate sight I see when scrolling through my news feeds online are individuals with some of the most interesting personal brands that have not become influential voices on social media. As unique and valuable as their content is, the inability to reach their ideal social media audience marks their failure. You can be a very talented person with sharable content; however, if you are not engaging with the type of people who would find your talent useful or informative, you will go unnoticed in the sea of brands on social networking sites. Perhaps the lack of visibility or engagement is due to influencers prioritizing their campaign or creative content first, before taking time to craft the perfect niche and find an audience that would support and uplift their personal brand.

Contrary to what you may believe, your target audience will not come running after you online because there is too much content to sift through. Instead, you are the one who is responsible for finding them and offering your value in plain sight. There are a few factors that can help you identify your ideal target audience. For instance, you can find them by identifying their age group, their average income, where they live, which technological devices they use, or the values that they believe in. There is no standard list of demographics that you need to include when finding your audience. Instead I recommend that you make your target profile requirements as specific to how an ideal customer would interact, perceive, find, and engage with your brand.

How to Find Your Target Audience Online

The success of your personal brand will depend on how well your content resonates with your target audience. There are many ways to find your audience online and create content that speaks to their needs and what they desire to see and experience from your brand. One way of finding your desired follower is to conduct an online survey that will provide you with a more detailed picture of who your customer is and what kind of social media behaviors and interests they have. A survey would allow you to pose the best questions to your community and receive the best responses to inform future content strategies or campaigns. If you already have a following, you can inbox your followers with a link to a quick survey form and request that they kindly fill it out (you could include an incentive with your request).

Your survey would address some pertinent questions regarding the preferences of your target audience. These could include questions such as:

- Which social media platform is your favorite to engage with?
- Which social media platform do you spend most of your time on?
- What hashtags do you usually search for?
- What kind of content do you prefer seeing on your news feeds or explore pages?
- Which celebrities or influencers do you follow on social media?
- What kind of content do you wish you saw more of online?
- Do you frequently read blog posts?
- What kind of information would make a blog post attractive to read?
- What type of relationship do you expect to have with an influencer or brand online?
- How can influencers engage with you on a more personal level?

Another way to find your desired target audience is to figure out your audience size. The audience size is the number of social media users that you intend to reach with your personal brand and marketing content. For instance, you may be interested in reaching young professional men and women in Chicago who are interested in property development. A quick search on Facebook would perhaps show you that the size of that audience on that particular platform consists of 600,000 people. For new influencers, a target audience as large as this may be too big of a bite to chew. Therefore, I recommend that you narrow your audience down more (make it more niche) to reach a more tailored and smaller audience in the beginning (perhaps you can target young professional men and women in Chicago who are interested in purchasing their first rental income property.

Lastly, you can find your ideal target audience by creating content tailored to their specific tastes. Creating tailored content requires the influencer to explore various types of content formats and media to gauge the interests of their audience. When it comes to sharing engaging content, the general rule of thumb is that influencers should not post more than one curated post per week, more than two promotional posts per week, and at least one engaging post per day. This content outline will help you post a variety of content that will show the kind of style, layouts, call-to-actions, and messaging that your ideal target audience loves. At the beginning of your journey, remember to compare and test your content campaigns to identify patterns of what works together and what elements are not as successful.

Even though your main objective may be to convert visitors into paying customers, your followers do not follow you to buy products from you every day. Therefore, your content plan must also include value that does not have a price tag on it. Ask yourself this question: how is my brand engaging with the target audience when it is not promoting sales content? This will allow you to create a content plan that focuses on maintaining a relationship with your audience through daily offers of valuable and engaging content without them having to feel compelled to make a purchase. You can offer value by making your social media pages a source for relevant information, inspiration, or entertainment. In this plan, you would include a variety of content, including polls, infographics, educational articles, tutorials, or motivational quotes and videos.

Social Media User Demographics Per Social Media Platform

Let us look through each social media platform and see what their statistical data shows about the social demographic present on each platform:

YouTube Demographics:

Active Monthly Users on YouTube

- Currently, YouTube has 2 billion monthly active users on its platform.

Age of Users

- Eight-one percent of individuals who use YouTube are between 15 to 25 years old;
- Seventy-one percent of individuals who use YouTube are between 26 to 35 years old;
- Sixty-seven percent of individuals who use YouTube are between 36 to 45 years old;
- Sixty-six percent of individuals who use YouTube are between 46 to 55 years old;
- Fifty-eight percent of individuals who use YouTube are 56 years and above.

Income

- Eighty-three percent of homes with a combined yearly revenue of less than $30,000 use YouTube;
- Eighty-one percent of homes with a combined yearly revenue between $30,000 and $60,000 use YouTube;
- Eighty percent of homes with a combined yearly revenue between $60,000 and $70,000 use YouTube;
- Eighty percent of homes with a combined yearly revenue between $70,000 and $80,000 use YouTube;
- Eighty-two percent of homes with a combined yearly revenue between $80,000 and $100,000 use YouTube;
- Eighty-nine percent of homes with a combined yearly revenue of more than $100,000 use YouTube.

Gender

- An estimate of 50% of YouTube users are female.

Time

- The average YouTube user spends approximately 11 minutes and 43 seconds every day on the platform.

Technological Devices

- An estimated 70% of YouTube users access the platform through their mobile devices such as smartphones.

The Most Followed YouTube Channels

- PewDiePie Channel: 102 million subscribers;
- Dude Perfect Channel: 47.5 million subscribers;
- Badabun Channel: 42.4 million subscribers.

Instagram Demographics:

Active Monthly Users on Instagram

- Currently, Instagram has 1 billion monthly active users on its platform.

Active daily users on Instagram

- Currently, Instagram has 500 million daily active users on its platform.

Age of Users

- Eighty-one percent of individuals who use Instagram are between 15 to 25 years old;
- Sixty-seven percent of individuals who use Instagram are between 18 to 29 years old;
- Forty-seven percent of individuals who use Instagram are between 30 to 49 years old;
- Twenty-three percent of individuals who use Instagram are between 50 to 64 years old;
- Eight percent of individuals who use Instagram are 65 years and above.

Income

- Forty-four percent of homes with a combined yearly revenue of less than $30,000 use Instagram;
- Forty-five percent of homes with a combined yearly revenue between $30,000 and $60,000 use Instagram;
- Thirty-six percent of homes with a combined yearly revenue between $60,000 and $70,000 use Instagram;
- Fifty-five percent of homes with a combined yearly revenue between $70,000 and $80,000 use Instagram;
- Forty-six percent of homes with a combined yearly revenue between $80,000 and $100,000 use Instagram;
- Sixty percent of homes with a combined yearly revenue of more than $100,000 use Instagram.

Gender

- An estimate of 51% of Instagram users are female;
- An estimate of 49% of Instagram users are male.

Time

- The average Instagram user spends approximately 53 minutes every day on the platform.

Statistics on Business and Shopping

- An estimated 71% of businesses in the United States have an Instagram account;
- Eighty-three percent of Instagram users confess to discovering information about new products and services while active on Instagram.

The Most Followed Instagram Pages

- Cristiano Ronaldo Page: 191 million followers;
- Ariana Grande Page: 163 million followers;

- Selena Gomez Page: 156 million followers.

Facebook Demographics:

Active Monthly Users on Facebook

- Currently, Facebook has 2.45 billion monthly active users on its platform.

Age of Users

- Eighty-six percent of individuals who use Facebook are between 18 to 29 years old;
- Seventy-seven percent of individuals who use Facebook are between 30 to 49 years old;
- Fifty-one percent of individuals who use Facebook are between 50 to 65 years old;
- Thirty-four percent of individuals who use Facebook are 65 years and above.

Income

- Eighty-five percent of homes with a combined yearly revenue of less than $30,000 use Facebook;
- Eighty-eight percent of homes with a combined yearly revenue between $30,000 and $60,000 use Facebook;
- Eighty-one percent of homes with a combined yearly revenue between $60,000 and $70,000 use Facebook;
- Eighty-eight percent of homes with a combined yearly revenue between $70,000 and $80,000 use Facebook;
- Eighty-six percent of homes with a combined yearly revenue between $80,000 and $100,000 use Facebook;
- Eighty-six percent of homes with a combined yearly revenue of more than $100,000 use Facebook.

Gender

- An estimate of 54% of Facebook users are female;
- An estimate of 46% of Facebook users are male.

Time

- The average Facebook user spends approximately 35 minutes every day on the platform.

Technological Devices

- An estimated 96% of Facebook users access the platform through their mobile devices such as smartphones;
- An estimated 25% of Facebook users access the platform through their laptops or desktop computers.

Most Followed Facebook Pages

- The Official Facebook Page: 214.6 million followers;
- Samsung Page: 159.8 million followers;
- Cristiano Ronaldo Page: 122.3 million followers.

Pinterest Demographics:

Active monthly Users on Pinterest

- Currently, Pinterest has 300 million monthly active users on its platform.

Age of Users

- Thirty-four percent of individuals who use Pinterest are between 18 to 29 years old;
- Thirty-five percent of individuals who use Pinterest are between 30 to 49 years old;
- Twenty-seven percent of individuals who use Pinterest are between 50 to 65 years old;
- Fifteen percent of individuals who use Pinterest are 65 years and above.

Income

- Eighteen percent of homes with a combined yearly revenue of less than $30,000 use Pinterest;
- Twenty-seven percent of homes with a combined yearly revenue between $30,000 and $74,999 use Pinterest;
- Forty-one percent of homes with a combined yearly revenue of more than $75,000 use Pinterest.

Gender

- An estimate of 70% of Pinterest users are female;
- An estimate of 30% of Pinterest users are male.

Time

- The average Pinterest user spends approximately 14.2 minutes per visit on the platform.

Technological Devices

- An estimated 80% of Pinterest users access the platform through their mobile devices such as smartphones.

Statistics on Business and Shopping

- On average, 90% of weekly Pinterest users will use the platform to inform their purchase decisions.
- Pinterest generates and drives 33% more referral traffic to online retail stores than Facebook.

TikTok Demographics:

Active Monthly Users on TikTok

- Currently, TikTok has 800 million monthly active users on its platform.

Active Daily Users on TikTok

- Currently, TikTok has 400 million daily active users in China and 45 million daily active users across the world on its platform.

Age of Users

- Twenty-seven percent of individuals who use TikTok are between 13 to 17 years old;
- Forty-two percent of individuals who use TikTok are between 18 to 24 years old;
- Sixteen percent of individuals who use TikTok are between 25 to 34 years old;
- Eight percent of individuals who use TikTok are between 35 to 44 years old;
- Three percent of individuals who use TikTok are between 45 to 54 years old;
- Four percent of individuals who use TikTok are 55 years and above.

Gender

- An estimate of 60% of TikTok users are female;
- An estimate of 40% of Pinterest users are male.

Time

- The average TikTok user spends approximately 52 minutes every day on the platform.

General Statistics on TikTok

- Forty-two percent of the revenue made by TikTok comes from the United States;
- Approximately 3.7 percent of the content shared on TikTok comes from brands;
- TikTok influencers who have a following of more than 2.5 million can charge upward of $800 for a sponsored post;
- TikTok hashtag challenges are the most popular type of advertisement on the platform;
- In November 2019, 68% of TikTok users confess to watching other people's videos frequently;
- In November 2019, 43% of TikTok users uploaded a duet;
- In November 2019, 50% of TikTok users shared someone else's video on another social media platform;
- Approximately 90% of TikTok users access the platform at least once a day.

Most Followed TikTok Pages

- Loren Gray Page: 36.5 million followers;
- Baby Ariel Page: 30 million followers;
- Zach King Page: 29 million followers.

Tactics on How to Locate Your Target Audience

All influencer desires to craft a niche in the specific industry they are interested in and build a strong and reputable personal brand. While this goal is admirable, there is a lot of behind-the-scenes preparation that takes place to be able to build a well-known brand. I believe the most crucial of preparations is locating your people online. Your people are your target audience, who will form a community that strengthens your brand's presence on various digital platforms. Without finding and connecting with your people, your brand will be discarded or undermined by those who are not interested.

Finding your target audience is not as simple as it may look. For instance, someone who purchases makeup may not necessarily enjoy watching video clips of makeup tutorials because truthfully, their interest is in finding good music online. Instead, you may find that your ideal customer is a makeup artist who enjoys playing around with different makeup techniques to improve their skills. As much as tools like Facebook Ads can help you filter a community, you will find that connecting to your people—your genuine, loyal supporters—will require various approaches. I would like to share these approaches with you as we come to the close of this book.

1. **Find a Distinct Need**

Locating a target audience is made simpler when you have identified a distinct need. To design a brand, content, or a product, without first identifying a need will compromise your search for the most suitable customer or follower. A need is an unmet desire or pain point that your ideal audience or customer cannot solve on their own. Sometimes customers are conscious about this need, and other times, they aren't; however, as soon as they engage with your brand, they realize that it is what they have been looking for all along. When you find a real need that you have the skills or talent to solve, you have found an opportunity to connect with an audience that will perceive you as valuable. You will know when you have located your target audience by the feedback or reviews that you receive, which communicate a transfer of value.

2. **Develop Your Solution**

Once you have found a distinct need that you believe that you can effectively solve, it is time to develop your solution. Remember that sometimes your ideal customer is unaware of their need, and therefore it is only through your presentation of a solution that they can realize what they have been missing out on. Expressing your value with words and not in actions or presenting a clear solution will prove ineffective in convincing audience members of your value. Developing your solution will require a sober understanding of your competitors (who may be other influencers or companies). Focus on what your competitors are missing in their offers or what they have overlooked. Even though this need may be obvious, there are so many companies who may have recognized it but never cared enough to solve it.

3. **Market Your Solution**

Now that you have a logical and creative solution, it is time to share it with others. Indeed, sharing is caring in this context because without expressing your solution, you are unable to help your target audience. Opening your brand's social media pages with a record low of zero followers is overwhelming; however, you must remember that you are carrying a solution. Through designing a strategic digital marketing strategy, you will be able to communicate this solution and gain followers in record-breaking time. The advantage that you will have entering the digital playing field is that you are not speaking to an entire population of young people, for example, but only to those who love pink shoelaces. This example may be humorous, but the message is clear: your solution should only be known by those you seek to provide with value. Remaining consistent with your brand and content will help you attract your people.

4. **Don't be afraid to Re-brand**

When your brand first launches its products or establishes its name on social media platforms, you will enter with a product or a brand identity that you perceive to be perfect. After gaining much experience, and observing the movement of competitors and cultural trends, you will find that the brand you started with can no longer provide a sustainable benefit or value offer to your target audience's ever-changing lifestyles. At some point, you will feel compelled to expand your interests, talents, or the direction your brand is going—all of which will be informed by the constantly changing interests and expectations of your target audience. In times like these, do not be afraid to focus on creating newer and fresher content, even if you start to explore other hobbies, skills, or topics. As your target audience grows, you will grow, and thus your personal brand should continue to grow as well. This will help you retain your audience and gain many more followers as you change.

Conclusion

Influencer marketing is an exciting addition to the broader marketing industry. It has offered regular people an opportunity to earn a living promoting products and services that they genuinely believe in and support. The role of an influencer might have been an unnecessary expenditure in previous years; however, much of the success of brand campaigns today is a result of using an influencer as a marketing tool. An influencer's value is not found in their background, who they know, or how much prior knowledge they have before entering the market. Instead, I find that an influencer's value is in how they can create strong relationships with communities of people online. The connection that influencers have with the customers that brands serve is what makes their role indispensable.

An influencer's success is built and tarnished by these online relationships that they build. When an influencer creates a brand that embraces their audience and shares valuable content, their power to influence customers' digital behavior increases. Conversely, when an influencer creates a brand that does not target the specific target audience that it seeks to engage with—and its content is of poor quality—the influencer has no power or influence in guiding customers to make purchase decisions online. In essence, an influencer's success or failure is seen in how much leverage they have built online and using this leverage to monetize their personal brands and make money through marketing opportunities.

I am grateful that I have seen such amazing examples of personal brands that were built well and generate millions of dollars per month. Nonetheless, I would be naive to assume that building a personal brand is as easy as how some of these influencers make it look. I also would not have had the opportunity to write this book if influencer marketing was straightforward and simple to set up. The knowledge that I have shared with you through these chapters is merely an introduction of influencer marketing. There is a lot more research, and dare I say experience, that you must gather to gain complete insight into the experience of becoming an influencer. I would like to take the opportunity now to reaffirm some of the potent lessons that I would like you to remember on your journey in becoming a thriving influencer.

Lesson One: Be Authentic

Those personal brands that become notable online and in society are undeniably authentic in how they express who they are and the value they proudly offer. There is no course that you can take to teach you how to be authentic to who you are. Being authentic is a decision that you need to make before building your personal brand. It is a decision that requires you to hold onto what you believe to be true about your personality, interest, talents, and ability to share who you are with others. Your authenticity is fundamental in allowing you to form meaningful connections with audiences online.

Lesson Two: Know Your Goals and Objectives

Every plan you make must have measurable goals that will help determine how close you are to the predetermined destination. Your goals are not created to sound informed or credible; they are, in fact, calculated milestones that you set that inform all of the necessary tactics of marketing your content or driving engagement onto your social media page. Without goals or objectives, your social media analytics will prove to be useless, and your social media advertising a waste of money. Therefore, start at the end by deciding what outcomes you hope to achieve with every plan or strategy that you make and then work with this guideline in place.

Lesson Three: Your Social Media Accounts Must Be Visually Appealing

In the context of digital marketing, content is king. Through your content, you can influence online customers and successfully convince them to make favorable purchasing decisions. Content that is of lower quality in terms of how it is displayed will negatively impact your brand's reputation. I remember a trend in previous years where celebrities were purposefully taking grainy photos and posting them on their pages (it was a trend which gained much popularity). As much I found these images odd and misplaced in our era, I noticed how much detail and editing went in to make these grainy images look desirable. The quality of an image is also determined by the amount of attention and detail that went in to make it tell an amazing story.

Lesson Four: Post Content Consistently

It is in the influencer's best interest to post content on to their social media accounts consistently. This lesson is so important because of how saturated social media feeds are becoming with content. It only takes a few days of being missing in action to become forgotten by your audience. As much as you might think that your brand's value is irreplaceable, it is frightening how easy it can and will be replaced. As much as you would nurture any personal relationship with a friend, you will need to nurture your relationship with your community.

There is never a time when your message becomes boring to a community of fans who love your content. Sometimes, a simple live stream allowing for an open discussion is as much content as you will need on that particular day. Your consistency in posting relevant and shareable content will, without any doubt, help you to grow your brand and level of engagement.

Lesson Five: Make Your Content SEO-friendly

As an influencer, I would encourage you to consider the bigger picture every now and again. Instead of solely looking at how well your content is performing on your Pinterest or Facebook page, I urge you to consider whether this content is discoverable on search engines such as Google. I say this because, as a personal brand, your number one priority is to reach as many members of your audience as you can (this will also allow you to generate more revenue from your pages down the line).

Therefore, with such a goal, it is important to understand that some of your audience has not heard about you yet, or perhaps they do not have an account on the social media platform that you are on. Thus, SEO should always be at the back of your mind as you create your content. You need to design content inclusive of all the common or trendy keywords that your potential follower may be searching for online. SEO will help you expand your reach and connect with audiences you would have never found on one or a few social media channels.

Lesson Six: Use a Variety of Content Formats

There is a reason why all of the social media platforms I have listed in this book offer various ways to create and share content. It is because these platforms understand how dynamic a user's page can look and feel having multiple content formats. For instance, an Instagram page with photography, stories, polls, and videos is far more interesting than an Instagram page, which only uses one format. Using a variety of content formats does not mean that your message should change or adjust within each type of content. It is possible to retain your message; however, changing how you express it. For instance, a chef influencer with a message of cooking simple, could post images of simple recipes, create stories documenting grocery shopping or preparing the dishes, and then post videos detailing the process of making simple and easy recipes.

Lesson Seven: Engage!

This lesson is emphasized the most throughout the book. It was not done to be a nag but to drive home the importance of engagement in an influencer's career. As much as I have given you many tips and tactics on building engagement on your social media channels, I understand that it is by far the most challenging process that all influencers will have to experience. Nonetheless, we have seen countless examples that it is possible to create a community of like-minded people who feel inspired to like, share, and comment on the influencer's posts. Becoming a pro at achieving engagement starts with ensuring that you are marketing to the right people—your people.

After that, it is up to your content's quality and relevance (and the effective use of calls-to-action) that create a culture of sharing responses, thoughts, or opinions on your posts. Engagement will be a constant metric that you measure throughout your social media channels. This single piece of data can cause brands to become enthusiastic about working with you on their campaigns. Do not give up on your efforts to build your engaged community—it has been done before, and you certainly can do it too.

Take Charge of Your Message

I shared with you at the beginning of this book that all of us—whether we are aware of it or not—carry a personal brand. If you do not believe me, look at the level of respect you have in your workspace or at home. By noticing how others perceive you, and whether or not they give you the respect that you deserve, you can measure the power of your personal and the level of influence it has to direct those around you to behave or act in certain ways. Reflecting on the power you possess to control the direction of your own life will also show you the amount of influence your message has. For instance, if you are passive and timid in your personal life, I can assure you that your message—however valuable it might be—goes unheard and unnoticed.

If anything at all, becoming an influencer is a journey in taking back the reins of your personal brand and ensuring that the message you carry about who you are and what you desire in this life is valued and supported. Even though there are many processes to follow when building your personal brand, the incentive it offers is to live your truth and allow other individuals similar to you to have the courage to live their truth. In essence, becoming an influencer is a call to leadership, and you are responsible for guiding your community members toward a more meaningful and enriching life. They can benefit from your brand through the many products and services you expose them to, which can add value to their lives. On the other hand, you, as the influencer, will also benefit from the marketing opportunities you receive due to your brand's value.

Influencer marketing ensures that all parties are winners and walk away with some form of reward from being a part of the influencer's network. With such an attractive marketing tool available to us, I cannot conceive a decline of the influencer marketing industry. I find that social media platforms are adjusting their algorithms in favor of this wave of influencer marketing. More than ever, anyone with an interesting hobby or talent can become the face of a brand. I hope that you have learned a significant amount of knowledge from this book, which will help you make wise decisions when building your personal brand and becoming an influencer. Remember to take charge of your message and lead your life in the most favorable direction for you. As you lead, you will find many others like you tailing behind.

References

55 *Video Marketing Statistics For 2020*. (n.d.). Biteable. https://biteable.com/blog/video-marketing-statistics/

30 *TikTok Statistics + 5 FAQs to Be Aware of in 2020*. (n.d.). 99firms. https://99firms.com/blog/tiktok-statistics/#gref

Armoo, T. (2019, September 6). *TikTok Tips & Tricks: 4 Ways to Create a Trending Hit*. Influencer Marketing Hub. https://influencermarketinghub.com/tiktok-tips-tricks-4-ways-to-create-a-trending-hit/

Atkinson, C. (2011, September 26). *Using Cross-Promotions & YouTube Video Collaborations to Increase Viewers: The YouTube Creator Playbook*. Tubular Insights. https://tubularinsights.com/cross-promotion-youtube-video-collaborations/

Audrezet, A., & De Kerviler, G. (2019, April). *How Brands Can Build Successful Relationships with Influencers*. Harvard Business Review. https://hbr.org/2019/04/how-brands-can-build-successful-relationships-with-influencers

Tosone, A. (2020, July 15). *Mistakes to Avoid When Pitching Brands as a Blogger*. Keep Calm and Chiffon. https://www.keepcalmandchiffon.com/blog/7/15/pitching-mistakes-to-avoid

Bailis, R. (2019, March 27). The State of Influencer Marketing: 10 Influencer Marketing Statistics to Inform Where You Invest. BigCommerce. https://www.bigcommerce.com/blog/influencer-marketing-statistics/#10-most-important-influencer-marketing-statistics-for-2020

Bogdan, A. (2019, August 19). *How to Find Your Target Audience on Social Media: 10 Tips to Follow*. PromoRepublic. https://promorepublic.com/en/blog/10-ways-find-audience-social-media/

Brown, L. (2020a, January 20). *Top 10 Best Free YouTube Video Editing Apps for iPhone & iPad [2020]*. Wondershare Filmora. https://filmora.wondershare.com/youtube-video-editing/edit-youtube-video-on-iphone.html

Brown, L. (2020b, May 18). *Best YouTube Video Editor Apps for Android [+How-tos]*. Wondershare Filmora.. https://filmora.wondershare.com/youtube-video-editing/edit-youtube-video-on-android.html

Prince, K. (2017, December 25). *5 Ways to Increase Engagement with Your Target Audience*. Jeff Bullas. https://www.jeffbullas.com/55-ways-to-increase-engagement-with-your-target-audience/

Cain, E. (2020, June 6). *How to Drive 3x More Traffic to Your Blog ith Pinterest.* Blogging Wizard. https://bloggingwizard.com/pinterest-traffic/

Cattoni, A. (2020, June 12). *Customer Avatar Exercise: How to Speak to Your Target Market.* Alex Cattoni. https://www.alexcattoni.com/customer-avatar-exercise-how-to-speak-to-your-target-market/

Clark, H. (2016, February 17). *5 Great Ways to Engage Your Audience on Instagram.* Hootsuite. https://blog.hootsuite.com/5-great-ways-to-engage-your-audience-on-instagram/

Cobain, D. (n.d.). *How Influencer Marketing Affects Consumer Buying Behaviour?* Miappi. https://miappi.com/how-influencer-marketing-affects-purchasing-behaviour/

Conlin, B. (2019, July 31). *How to Reach Your Target Audience.* Business News Daily. https://www.businessnewsdaily.com/15229-reach-your-target-audience.html

Cooper, P. (2019, August 1). *How to Make Money on Instagram: 3 Foolproof Strategies.* Hootsuite. https://blog.hootsuite.com/how-to-make-money-on-instagram/

Cover, L. (2019, June 5). *10 Pinterest Statistics Marketers Must Know in 2019.* Sprout Social. https://sproutsocial.com/insights/pinterest-statistics/

Cronin, N. (2018, October 4). *A Simple Guide to Instagram Influencer Marketing in 2020.* Hopper HQ. https://www.hopperhq.com/blog/instagram-influencer-marketing-2020/

Cyca, M. (2020, April 28). *9 Ideas for Creative TikTok Videos that Will Engage Your Followers.* Hootsuite. https://blog.hootsuite.com/tiktok-video-ideas/

Digital Marketer. (n.d.). The Ultimate Guide to Digital Marketing [PDF]. In *Digital Marketer.* https://www.digitalmarketer.com/digital-marketing/assets/pdf/ultimate-guide-to-digital-marketing.pdf

DMI, S. (2018, July 10). *Social Media Demographics Guide for Digital Marketers.* Digital Marketing Institute. https://digitalmarketinginstitute.com/blog/social-media-demographics-guide-for-digital-marketers

Elliott, N. (2015, September 15). *How Does Your Brand Stack Up on Facebook, Twitter, And Instagram?* Forrester. https://go.forrester.com/blogs/15-09-15-how_does_your_brand_stack_up_on_facebook_twitter_and_instagram/

Emma. (2019, March 7). *How to Find Brands to Work with as a Microinfluencer.* Emma's Edition. https://www.emmasedition.com/2019/03/find-brands-to-work-with-blogger.html

Evans, D. (2011). *Social media marketing: The next generation of business engagement.* Wiley Publishing, Inc. https://www.pauladaunt.com/books/Social%20Media%20Marketing.pdf

Fitzpatrick, P. (2017, February 23). *How to Create Beautiful Pinterest Pins.* Tailwind. https://blog.tailwindapp.com/beautiful-pinterest-pins/

Foster, J. (2018, June 6). *How to use Pinterest to Drive High-Volume Traffic on Auto-Pilot.* Marketing Land. https://marketingland.com/how-to-use-pinterest-to-drive-high-volume-traffic-on-auto-pilot-241453

Galipeau, L. (2019, October 30). *Four Pinterest Strategies to Increase Your Traffic.* Pinterest Traffic Builder. http://pinteresttrafficbuilder.com/four-pinterest-strategies-to-increase-your-traffic/

Gander, M. (2014). Managing your personal brand. *Perspectives: Policy and Practice in Higher Education, 18*(3), 99–102. https://doi.org/10.1080/13603108.2014.913538

Gertsberg, P. (2019, April 10). *Social media monetisation: Everything you need to know.* Disciple. https://www.disciplemedia.com/monetising-your-community/social-media-monetisation/

Get Smarter. (n.d.). *Personal Brand Guide* [PDF]. https://www.getsmarter.com/blog/wp-content/uploads/2016/12/GetSmarter_Personal_Brand_Guide.pdf

Gotter, A. (2020, January 5). *The Ideal YouTube Channel Art Size & Best Practices.* Snappa. https://blog.snappa.com/youtube-channel-art-size/

Grin Admin. (n.d.). *9 Ways to Get Your YouTube Channel Noticed!* Grin. https://grow.grin.co/9-ways-to-get-your-youtube-channel-noticed/

Henneberry, R. (n.d.). *The Ultimate Guide to Digital Marketing.* DigitalMarketer. https://www.digitalmarketer.com/digital-marketing/

History.com Editors. (2019, October 28). *The Invention of the Internet.* HISTORY. https://www.history.com/topics/inventions/invention-of-the-internet

How Brands Are Partnering with Facebook Influencers. (n.d.). Mediakix. https://mediakix.com/blog/facebook-influencers-brand-marketing-partnerships/

How to Market Your Business with Pinterest [PDF]. (2014). AWeber. https://6elrmjmsbs335jwbeybarrry-wpengine.netdna-ssl.com/wp-content/uploads/2014/08/Marketing-Your-Business-with-Pinterest.pdf

How to Master the Art of Instagram Collaboration. The Design Twins. https://www.thedesigntwins.com/how-to-master-instagram-collaboration/

How to Pitch Yourself as an Influencer to Brands [+Templates]. (2019, September 4). Zine. https://blog.zine.co/how-to-pitch-yourself-as-an-influencer-to-brands

Hoyt, B. (2020, January 10). *How to Make Money on Pinterest in 2020 (Earn $1,000 Extra Per Month!).* Millennial Money Man. https://millennialmoneyman.com/how-to-make-money-on-pinterest/

Influencer Marketing Admin. (2019a, January 11). *How to Create an Award Winning Influencer Media Kit.* Influencer Marketing Hub. https://influencermarketinghub.com/influencer-media-kit/

Influencer Marketing Admin. (2019b, January 18). *What is TikTok? What you need to know about the new Musical.ly.* Influencer Marketing Hub. https://influencermarketinghub.com/what-is-tiktok/

Influencer Marketing Admin. (2019c, October 28). *The Ultimate YouTube Influencer Marketing Guide.* Influencer Marketing Hub. https://influencermarketinghub.com/youtube-influencer-marketing-guide/

Influencer Marketing Admin. (2020a, April 16). *How to Feature on TikTok's "For You" Page.* Influencer Marketing Hub. https://influencermarketinghub.com/tiktok-for-you-page/

Irina Weber. (2018, December 12). *6 Ways to Use IGTV for Business.* Social Media Examiner. https://www.socialmediaexaminer.com/6-ways-use-igtv-business/#:~:text=The%20IGTV%20platform%20is%20designed

Keser, A. (n.d.). *How to Be Successful on YouTube in 10 Easy Steps.* Blue Fountain Media. https://www.bluefountainmedia.com/blog/how-to-be-successful-on-youtube

The 2020 Social Media Demographics Guide. (n.d.). Khoros. https://khoros.com/resources/social-media-demographics-guide

Lumley, M. (2019, March 14). *How to Build a Successful Pinterest Marketing Strategy: A Marketer's Guide.* Social Bakers. https://www.socialbakers.com/blog/pinterest-marketing-strategy

Masek-Kelly, E. (2018, April 17). *3 Ways to Monetize Social Media That Actually Work.* Social Media Today. https://www.socialmediatoday.com/news/3-ways-to-monetize-social-media-that-actually-work/521474/

Mattie. (2017, August 15). *The Truth About Brand Partnerships & How to Get Them.* Mattie James. https://mattiejames.com/how-to-get-brand-partnerships/

(n.d.). *TikTok Influencer Marketing: How to Work with TikTok Influencers.* Mediakix. https://mediakix.com/influencer-marketing-resources/tik-tok-influencer-marketing/

(n.d.). Top *10 TikTok Trends in 2019.* Mediakix. https://mediakix.com/blog/tik-tok-trends/

Mohsin, M. (2020a, May 11). *10 Youtube Stats Every Marketer Should Know in 2020 [Infographics].* Oberlo. https://www.oberlo.com/blog/youtube-statistics#:~:text=YouTube%20has%202%20billion%20users%20worldwide.

Mohsin, M. (2020b, July 3). *10 TikTok Statistics That You Need to Know in 2020 [Infographics]].* Oberlo.. https://www.oberlo.co.za/blog/tiktok-statistics

Moore, A. (2018, January 2). *How to Build an Engaged Instagram Community.* Tailwind. https://blog.tailwindapp.com/5-ways-to-develop-a-killer-community-on-instagram/

Mtalii, E. (2020, July 7). *10 Proven Ways How to Make Money on TikTok in 2020! | Kenyan YouTuber.* Eva Mtalii. https://www.evamtalii.com/10-proven-ways-how-to-make-money-on-tiktok-in-2020-kenyan-youtuber/

Nazeer, A. (2019, December 10). *How to Find the Best Times to Pin on Pinterest for More Traffic.* Shemeansblogging. https://shemeansblogging.com/how-to-find-the-best-times-to-pin/

Newberry, C. (2019, October 2). *How to Advertise on Facebook in 2020: The Definitive Facebook Ads Guide.* Hootsuite. https://blog.hootsuite.com/how-to-advertise-on-facebook/

Noyes, D. (2019, January 8). *Top 20 Facebook Statistics - Updated January 2019.* Zephoria Digital Marketing. https://zephoria.com/top-15-valuable-facebook-statistics/

. *5 Tips for Using Instagram Carousel Ads.* Online Advertising School. https://www.onlineadvertisingschool.com/lesson/5-tips-for-using-instagram-carousel-ads/

Facebook Monetization: The What, Why, Where, and How. (n.d.) Oberlo.. https://www.oberlo.com/ebooks/monetize/make-money-facebook

How to Monetize Instagram for Your Business. (n.d.) Oberlo.. https://www.oberlo.com/ebooks/monetize/monetize-instagram

Pearce, K. (n.d.). *Build a Personal Brand That Matters* [PDF]. https://www.diygenius.com/Build-A-Personal-Brand-That-Matters.pdf

Phillips, A. (2020, February 6). *23 Ways to Easily Increase Instagram Engagement in 2020.* Falcon.Io. https://www.falcon.io/insights-hub/topics/social-media-strategy/21-tips-increase-instagram-engagement/

Pratt, K. (2018, February 24). *How to Create a Lookalike Audience on Facebook.* Boostability. https://www.boostability.com/how-to-create-a-lookalike-audience-on-facebook/

Quoc, M. (2018, March 12). *Why Influencers Are Essential After Facebook's News Feed Update*. Mention. https://mention.com/en/blog/facebook-influencer-marketing/

Rothman, N. (n.d.). *How to Build a Relationship-Based Influencer Marketing Strategy*. Sideqik. https://www.sideqik.com/influencer-marketing/relationship-based-influencer-marketing

Sailer, B. (2019, October 2). *13 Ways to Create It That Succeeds on Social Media*. CoSchedule Blog. https://coschedule.com/blog/shareable-content/

Sehl, K. (2020, May 7). *20 Important TikTok Stats Marketers Need to Know in 2020*. Hootsuite. https://blog.hootsuite.com/tiktok-stats/#:~:text=TikTok%20has%20a%20reputation%20for

Shannon. (2015, October 12). *How to Find and Engage Your Target Audience*. AddThis Academy. https://www.addthis.com/academy/how-to-find-and-engage-your-target-audience/

Sidewalker Daily. (2018, September 26). *10 Expert Tips to Pitch as a Micro-Influencer*. Sidewalker Daily. https://sidewalkerdaily.com/pitch-as-a-micro-influencer/#close-it

Singal, N. (2020, April 15). *How to Make Money on TikTok*. Business Today. https://www.businesstoday.in/technology/news/how-tiktokers-are-making-money-on-the-platform/story/390751.html

Smith, J. (n.d.). *3 Ways Facebook Advertising Impacts Your SEO Results*. OuterBox. https://www.outerboxdesign.com/search-marketing/seo-tips/facebook-advertising-seo-impact

Smoteks, H. (2020, May 29). *15 Tips for Your Fan Page - Updated May 2020*. Linkody's Blog. https://blog.linkody.com/digital-agency/facebook-seo

Stark, A. (2020, January 3). *10 Ways to Get More Followers on TikTok*. Web Daytona. https://webdaytona.com/10-ways-to-get-more-followers-on-tiktok/

Stearn, M. (2019, May 23). *How to Enable Monetization on YouTube*. Storyblocks. https://blog.storyblocks.com/creators/how-to-enable-youtube-monetization/

Thames, M. (2019, August 21). *Mistakes to Avoid When Pitching Brands*. Happily Ever Natural. https://www.happilyevernatural.com/blogging-tips/mistakes-to-avoid-when-pitching-brands-3/

Vest, J. (2018, January 4). *15 Tips for Growing Your YouTube Channel*. Social Media Examiner. https://www.socialmediaexaminer.com/15-tips-growing-youtube-channel/

Worb, J. (2020, August 3). *The Ultimate Guide to Instagram Reels*. Later Blog. https://later.com/blog/instagram-reels/

Create or Edit Channel Art - YouTube Help. (n.d.) Support.Google.Com. https://support.google.com/youtube/answer/2972003?co=GENIE.Platform%3D Desktop&hl=en

Editing. (n.d.) Youtube Creator Academy. https://creatoracademy.youtube.com/page/lesson/editing#strategies-zippy-link-3

Zovitsky, K. (2018, April 20). *Instagram Marketing Strategy*. Conversion Advantage. https://www.conversionadvantage.com/instagram-marketing-strategy/

www.ingramcontent.com/pod-product-compliance
Lightning Source LLC
Chambersburg PA
CBHW031433210526
45464CB00005B/2183